It's Personal

GROWING YOUR LEADERSHIP, IMPACT, AND RELATIONSHIPS

ALLISON CLARKE, CSP

It's Personal:
Growing Your Leadership, Impact, and Relationships

Copyright @2024 by Allison Clarke

Published by Charles Freeman Publishers

Paperback ISBN: 978-0-9897330-0-7
Hardcover ISBN: 978-0-9897330-2-1

Every attempt has been made to properly source all quotes and attribute all research.

Printed in the United States of America

First Edition

For you, reading this . . .

Contents

CHAPTER 3:

PERSONALIZE YOUR BUSINESS IMPACT

CHAPTER 4:

PERSONALIZE YOUR APPRECIATION

CHAPTER 5:

PERSONALIZE YOUR FEEDBACK

Introduction

"My mission in life is not merely to survive, but to thrive; and to do so with some passion, some compassion, some humor, and some style."

— *Maya Angelou*

One of my first jobs was at a restaurant in Oregon where the owner tried to recreate the spirit of the old TV show, "Cheers." He envisioned a safe haven, a place where people could come together, be themselves, and leave their daily concerns behind. Having watched the show as a kid, I understood the assignment. I had to learn people's names, listen to their stories, remember their preferences, and interact as though we were friends.

Great to see you, Randy. Can I grab you a Coors Light?
Jackie, it's been weeks. How was your daughter's wedding?
Hey Sid, are you in the mood for french fries again?

These simple statements put huge smiles on people's faces. I'd watch their eyes soften and shoulders relax, as they'd take a deep breath for what seemed like the first time that day. Clearly, they were hungry for positive interaction, perhaps more than the food itself. When people were under our roof, they felt heard and seen, which by the way, made the restaurant financially successful. Our secret sauce had nothing to do with food. It was about making people feel special.

Working for that business gave me energy. It grew my confidence, opened doors for my future, and it often made me laugh. It also taught me that everyone deserves to be recognized, welcomed, and served. We really have no idea what is going on in their lives. We also have no idea how powerful we really are, nor do we realize how much our surroundings dictate our moods and aspirations, like the restaurant did for me and countless others.

From there, my interest in personalized engagement only grew. It seemed almost too easy to blow people away with easy acts of kindness. If a sincere handshake or wave could dramatically shift how people feel, I wondered what else could be done to honor people to the fullest extent. Was there a more "studious" approach to make people feel good? I became determined to find out.

In spring 2010, I started Allison Clarke Consulting and began a research study into top-level customer service. Naturally, I found myself in the hospitality industry, the Ritz Carlton and Four Seasons hotels to be precise. I thought they could teach me their secrets, the reason they were viewed as superior.

How did they get their impeccable reputation for customer happiness?

Why do people all over the world pay top-dollar to stay there?

As it turned out, their service wasn't much of a secret. It actually wasn't different from anything I'd seen before. Prior to starting my business, I'd spent 16 years working at the Dale Carnegie Corporation, where I moved up the ranks to become a "Top 25 Master Trainer." You might have heard of Mr. Carnegie, he was a bestselling author of *How to Win Friends and Influence People*, which taught his philosophies for success.

In those years as a Carnegie trainer, I witnessed thousands of people learn how to turn their focus onto other people to better relate to their most important relationships – and every time, it shaped their leadership and helped their business too. Their services became known as superior, and their style of relating became admired.

That's precisely what I saw at the Ritz and Four Seasons. They were using leadership principles, seamlessly applied to each customer by a well-trained team. They were also using soft skills, which basically mean people skills. They're called "soft" because they're non-technical, yet how you interact with others is crucial to business success.

When you pull into the Four Seasons, you're greeted by a valet who asks a series of questions about your visit. Your answers are conveyed to the front desk, so they can greet you appropriately and further personalize your experience at the property. They also have files for each guest. They know why you're visiting, where you're going, and they know your special needs – oat milk with your coffee, ice bucket delivered at 6:30 p.m., white noise for sound sleep, along with extra pillows. Afterwards, they send you an extensive survey to see if your expectations were met. They stay in touch, and they do it well.

This is what five-star service entails, and it happens because the hotel team works together. These premiere hotels exemplify a "we" mentality. They are also masterful at communication.

Knowing how to treat the customer is only half the battle. Every corporation faces the challenge of interpersonal conflict, poor leadership, and miscommunication. These are the elephants in the room at every organization, and when they aren't properly cared for and acknowledged, there's a price to pay. Can you believe $1.2 trillion is lost annually in U.S. businesses because of unsuccessful communication practices?[1]

> $1.2 trillion is lost annually in U.S. businesses because of unsuccessful communication practices.

The reason is avoidance. People think facing communication issues means casting shame and blame, and making people feel uncomfortable. That's why businesses tend to fixate on the numbers, enforce more rules, or make operational goals more pressing than relational ones. They want to intellectualize, when they need to get intentional about how they're relating companywide.

Most problems in business are people problems. Their solutions cannot be solved in a spreadsheet. They require better self-care, refined leadership, and personalized communication. This special care must be taken each time we interact with anyone, including ourselves.

Think of it like this . . .

We live in a world that personalizes everything to our liking. It's what shapes our identity and makes us feel special, like we matter. Take etsy.com, for example. The website is built on celebrating the unique nature of every crafter, creative, and community. Whatever you can dream up, you'll likely find and it's why this site has continued to thrive. People don't go there to buy standard items and sell standard goods. They shop there for treasures that remind them of who they are and what makes them tick.

Our styles shape everything around us. Look around and notice how you've personalized your own life.

- Is your bedroom or office customized to your specific taste?
- Is your tea, coffee, or beverage made exactly how you like it?
- Is your music list personalized, along with your book collection?

Everything these days is personalized. Insurance policies are designed to meet your unique needs, as is your home, car, vacations, jewelry, nails, tattoos, streaming services, makeup, vitamins, fantasy football league, collector's items, and of course, your phone.

Name three things around you that celebrate your unique preferences and interests. Name the reasons they make you happy.

Here's the thing: It takes effort to hone a collection of your favorite things, and we don't think twice about doing it. Now answer this: When have you taken the same effort to personalize your communication with others?

That means your focus must expand, and your awareness has to include what other people require and desire, which can (and does) change.

This has been my lifelong mission—to learn what humans need to thrive in life and at work. I don't claim to know what's best for all people, though I do know that people crave connection. As I write this book, the news is fairly doom and gloom. There are daily reports of increasing depression, anxiety, isolation, suicide, gun violence, destruction of the Earth, and social division. Fear is growing, along with negativity and hopelessness.

We each need to find what we can control.

One of those things is the kindness you can spread, which includes being kind to yourself. Keep in mind, though, kindness isn't a one-way venture. While practicing the skill of honoring your fellow human, you get rewarded too. It doesn't take much time or effort either, and when these acts are complete, it can mend the fabric of humanity and soothe our weary hearts.

That's why this book was written.

It's Personal: Growing Your Leadership, Impact, and Relationships is a love letter to humanity and a guidebook for both business and life. Its core message is succinct:

Quality of life isn't found in your resume, income, or social status, it's about your ability to make people feel valued, while also honoring your own wants and needs.

There's power in a simple hug, smile, text, phone call, or wave. Do you realize these gestures have stopped people from ending their lives? Your presence can be enough to keep someone's hope alive – not only in their lives, but also their careers.

This book is designed to improve your work relationships and boost your profits in business. Since automation and remote work became the norm, everyone's scrambling to figure out employee engagement. How do you have cohesive teams, when they're scattered on screens and in multiple locations?

A Gallup report says people feel good about their jobs when they have close and supportive relationships at work. It makes sense, even with remote workers. Engaged employees consistently deliver better outcomes, regardless of industry, company size, or economic climate. Yet the numbers are somewhat bleak:

Only 23% of employees worldwide and 32% in the U.S. are currently considered "engaged."[2]

Who's responsible for fixing this? Well, the leader's primary role is to ensure employment engagement, though it takes a collective effort. Throughout these pages, I'll reveal what my clients and other companies are doing to successfully and efficiently address these issues.

Please realize something – this book is short for a reason. Eye-tracking studies show that people spend 26 seconds, on average, reading a piece of content.[3] We have frazzled and fragmented attention spans, which requires short and compelling content.

I also value your time and want you to get quick results.

If you can spend five minutes reading and applying even one of my principles, it can shift a mediocre day into a mind-blowing one. They can spark your career overnight and strengthen your relationships, as they've done for many years for myself and others.

Here's how this book is set up:

Chapter 1:

Personalize Your Wellness is about taking better care of yourself. You know how the airlines tell us to put on our air mask first before assisting others? That's why we're focusing on you first. I promise you won't find typical self-help strategies in this chapter, but rather unique ideas to make inner peace and mental health your priority.

Chapter 2:

Personalize Your Leadership begins by reframing your definition of leadership. A big title or fancy salary doesn't make a leader. It's a person's ability to connect with people and to inspire them, or at least to make them feel heard and seen. Those are the rare and impactful leadership skills you'll learn in this chapter.

Chapter 3:

Personalize Your Business Impact is meant to be an eye-opener. We are always presenting in our jobs and careers. Each word matters, as do the steps we take to build our networks and sell our products or services. But how do you stand out in the sea of digital noise? That's what this chapter provides!

Chapter 4:

Personalize Your Appreciation is about fostering genuine connections based on respect. You'll be encouraged to find people's favorite receiving styles, give thanks in respectful and meaningful ways, and to acknowledge those who might not be seen or heard much, but deserve to be showcased and honored.

Chapter 5:

Personalize Your Feedback might sound a little scary, but that's only because feedback has been unfairly deemed negative. When practiced regularly, positively, and skillfully, it can be the catalyst people need to grow their relationships, reach their goals, and achieve new levels of self-awareness.

If you remember one thing from this book, let it be this: We have no idea what is going on in people's lives. We also have no idea how powerful we really are. This book now gives you a chance to discover.

Through personalization, you'll soon be standing out, feeling creative, loving yourself, clicking with others, making breakthroughs, and becoming known as a leader who improves the quality of business and everyday life.

Christina reminds you take care of yourself first.

Chapter 1

Personalize Your Wellness

"Today, I love myself enough to not only make a promise to myself, but I love myself enough to keep that promise."

— *Steve Maraboli*

When you look at your phone and see the battery is running low, how do you typically respond? If you're like most people, you freak out a little and instantly seek a place to recharge. The same thing happens behind the wheel. If your gas tank gets low, your confidence and sense of security won't be as strong, until the gauge says it's full again.

This chapter invites you to view yourself with the same importance (and urgency) as your devices and vehicles, which means you have to get honest about:

- how you really feel
- what's going through your mind
- what you actually need
- how much you can truly give to others

This inner focus might seem uncomfortable at first, yet it's essential for building on every aspect of your life, leadership, and legacy. You must place yourself at the center, as if *your* battery is keeping you alive, because it is!

That's why this chapter exists–to keep your energy and intentions in check, so that your best self can emerge and engage with life meaningfully. After all, personalization starts with you, so let's get you going in a smart direction.

1

Witness Yourself Honestly

On page one of my second book, *The Kindness Habit*, I asked readers to pretend there are hidden cameras filming them from the moment they open their eyes, until they crawl into bed at night. This information is (hypothetically) collected and given to them as a review of what they did, what they said, and what they thought.

After reviewing their day, they were asked to assess:

- *How much am I worrying?*
- *What kind of foods am I eating?*
- *What judgments do I have?*
- *How much time am I spending online?*
- *How often do I show appreciation?*
- *How many risks do I take?*
- *How honest am I with others?*
- *Where do I spend my money?*
- *How often do I offer or ask for help?*
- *What am I doing for others?*

This exercise provides a chance to self-reflect and see yourself in raw form. It also gives you keen insight into thoughts and behaviors you might want to change, but have been minimizing or avoiding. We all have inklings, if not striking clarity, on what's needed for our personal and professional evolution. Our bodies constantly give us signals, however it can be easy to deny and ignore them, rather than acknowledge a change is being requested.

Please know these imaginary hidden cameras aren't there just to trigger your inner critic. They are meant to reflect your brilliance, beauty, and uniqueness.

- Do you realize how important you are to other people?
- Can you see your compassion and kindness?
- Do you identify your greatness and strengths?
- Can you see how much your contributions and ideas matter?
- Can you see the mark you left in other people's lives?

This positive view of yourself is essential to your wellbeing, as is knowing your areas for growth. It's all too easy to focus on what you don't like about yourself. That's why most people have to take 15 selfies to find that *one* angle they like – which prompts me to ask:

Do you say mean things to yourself that you'd never say to anyone else? I do it too, and when I ask this question, 19 out of 20 people (if not everyone) raise their hand. It's always a bonding moment, where we collectively sigh, knowing that everyone has an inner critic that must be tempered.

The narrator in our minds can be scary. This is why I give my training participants monster finger puppets. You know the plastic kind you place on your finger? It's a reminder of the persistent little voice inside our heads that can go unchecked. I also give them Silly Putty and stress balls, so they can decompress and remember to be kind to themselves.

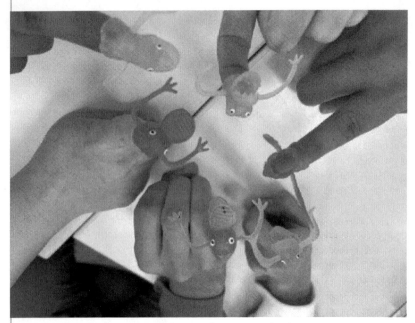

Workshop participants playing with their monsters.

According to research from Dr. Fred Luskin of Stanford University, human beings have approximately 60,000 thoughts *per day*, and 90% of these are repetitive.[1] This means we need regular inventory checks to see what's swirling around up there! Otherwise, we run on thoughts that do not serve who we want to be.

When's the last time you examined your thoughts?

Harvard Business School professor Gerald Zaltman says, "Probably 95% of all cognition, all the thinking that drives our decisions and behaviors, occurs unconsciously—and that includes consumer decisions."[2] Can you believe that? This means we need to take seriously what our brain may be saying without our full consent.

Consider this powerful quote attributed to many: "Don't speak negatively about yourself, even as a joke. Your body doesn't know the difference. Words are energy and cast spells that's why it's called spelling. Change the way you speak about yourself and you can change your life. What you're not changing you're also choosing."

Remember, your brain only knows what you tell it. When you're hard on yourself, your brain absorbs it as reality. When you're gentle with yourself, your brain sees it as the concrete truth. It's like your mind is a sponge, soaking up the messages you feed it. It's amazing to think how much control we can have just by choosing a positive narrative.

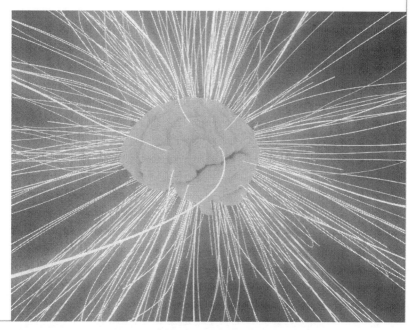

2

Imagine the Finish Line

When I've had to manage a stressful situation, end an intimate relationship, make a big move, or get through a tough race, I always imagine what it will be like to reach the finish line.

For instance, as I write this, I'm preparing to rent my place and move. The logistics of this transition are tedious, but I keep imagining the gorgeous sea of Aspen trees located outside my (new) bedroom window. I did the same thing when I left Bend, Oregon, for Fort Collins, Colorado. I thought about eating Krazy Karl's pizza and sipping Fat Tire beer on the patio with my daughter.

Visualization is crucial to the success of elite athletes. Studies show that mental imagery improves an athlete's motor skills in competition, as well as their ability to learn new skills during training.

Emily Cook, a three-time Olympian in freestyle skiing, has an approach that involves recording mental scenarios, such as standing atop the hill, feeling the wind on her neck, and hearing the crowd. She insists you must smell, hear, and feel to fully prepare the body and mind to succeed.[3] When your brain can grasp the full experience, it also reduces anxiety.

"If my mind can conceive it, and my heart can believe it—then I can achieve it."

— Muhammad Ali

Feel the Ideal Feeling

It's important to think about how you want to perform, but it also helps to visualize how you want *others* to feel. When I'm overwhelmed with work, I take the focus off myself and visualize how these principles enhance people's lives. Essentially, I think about the impact of my actions, instead of the stress of getting it done.

For instance, if you're terrified of public speaking, you could see yourself adding value to your audience. It also helps to visualize people walking away feeling energized and inspired by your message. Think about why you need to do this presentation. Both of these approaches will help you get into a healthy frame of mind—and there's science behind the results.

Did you know about 70% of the Earth's surface is covered in water, while roughly 60% of the human body is made up of water?[4,5] With these water percentages being so high, it makes Dr. Masaru Emoto's research on water crystals especially compelling. His experiments showed a change in the molecular structure of water, as a result of positive or negative vibrations from words or music. For example, water exposed to both written and spoken words such as "love" or "gratitude" created a visually pleasing, snowflake-like structure, while words exposed to words like "I hate you" formed ugly and distorted shapes.[6]

So if words have an effect on the shape of water crystals, and we're made up of 60% water, the words we hear, think, and speak have a profound effect too. That means it's perfectly okay, if not encouraged, to talk to your houseplants or really anything that you consume. Infuse it with love and appreciation and watch how things transpire.

4

Speak Your Gratitude

Practicing gratitude is an ingrained habit for me. Each time I give thanks, it shifts me into a better place. That's why I perked up recently at a Rotary meeting when given a tip for increased happiness:

Vocalize what brings you joy.

Saying it out loud sends a signal to your brain that triggers endorphins. I've implemented this advice and make a point to audibly give thanks for the sunrise outside my bedroom window, elk in the yard, tulips in the garden, or the creative foam pattern on the top of my latte. This helps our brains to further savor the goodness and joy. Like when I crawl into bed, I actually say, "Ahh, I love it here!"

Gratitude can be harder to conjure when sickness or pain strikes. We often forget how amazing our bodies are, until they start acting up. Right? It often takes a health scare for us to show our bodies the love and attention it needs, but you can change this starting today.

Let your body know it's doing a great job. Even if you're not feeling well, there are parts of your body that are doing well. Consider every limb, muscle, and organ as a gift that you are thankful to have received.

- *Thank you, feet, for getting me around.*
- *Thank you, heart, for pumping away.*
- *Thank you, lungs, for giving me breath.*
- *Thank you, hands, for the work I do.*
- *Thank you, brain, for helping me think.*

Another way to unleash an attitude of gratitude is to think of the best compliment you've received. How did it make you feel?

You're not alone if this question takes time to answer. It's not uncommon to have to plunge your memory, however, try to recall both the compliment and the impact it had on you.

I'll never forget in my 20s, while training to be a Dale Carnegie instructor, Mike Stack gave me invaluable feedback. He said I was a natural, which instantly boosted my confidence. At the time, I was coaching mostly men in their 40s. To hear that my skills came across as genuine and effortless gave me validation. It shifted something inside of me, where I no longer questioned my competency.

I owned and became grateful for my natural gifts, and aimed to use them wisely.

Remember, what leaves our lips can linger throughout time, for better or worse. A kind word can help retain employees and customers, and save a friendship; just as an unkind word can burn a bridge or make someone leave. Think of words like they're in a tube of toothpaste. Once they've been squeezed out, there's no way to put them back in. That means we must choose words of gratitude towards ourselves and everyone, and not be afraid to say them out loud.

Find Your
Life Path

We cannot underestimate the impact of our words, nor can we downplay the importance of finding our life path. One of my vendors knows this to be true.

Joshua Neumann, founder of Kind Lips

Joshua Neumann grew up in Oklahoma. He went to college to be a teacher in Wisconsin, and then shifted his course to Minnesota, where he became one of Minneapolis's top residential real estate brokers. Despite his good health, loving family, and tangible assets, something was missing from his life.

One day, when Josh was in between client meetings, he noticed the tube of lip balm resting in his hand. That's when time stood still and Josh became fixated on the idea of making his own blend. That evening, he began mixing ingredients in his kitchen, until he eventually found an all-natural formula made to nourish and protect lips.

Josh kept his mom in the loop of his progress. They'd brainstorm names for his product and discuss his new venture. One day, she called Josh at 6 a.m. to say she had a vivid dream about Josh and his sister, where they were still in grade school. As a punishment for arguing with each other, Josh had to sit in a classroom and repeatedly write:

The law of kindness is on my lips.
The law of kindness is on my lips.
The law of kindness is on my lips.
The law of kindness is on my lips.
The law of kindness is on my lips.
The law of kindness is on my lips.

This story gave Josh chills, and it felt affirming. His mom added, "If you need a name for your business, you should call it Kind Lips." In 2019, Josh left real estate, did what his mom said, and never looked back.

Kind Lips is one of my cherished partners today. I buy tubes by the thousands and give them away to strangers, friends, and clients. It's not just the product that's superb, it's the reminder the lip balm provides: Words matter.

Josh backs his kindness mission by giving away 20% to groups that prevent bullying and suicide, and advocate for mental health.[7] He's also now a role model for what it means to personalize and pivot your life. He demonstrates how your work can serve a more satisfying purpose.

When you speak kindly to yourself and others, and you seek new paths of curiosity, that's when you find roads that were meant just for you.

Joshua Neumann's Self Kindness Pledge.

NAME:

- ☑ I am confident in my abilities.
- ☑ I am valuable and worthy of love.
- ☑ I can choose to work hard.
- ☑ I am kind and want to care for other people.
- ☑ I am able to overcome challenges.
- ☑ I love myself.
- ☑ I am a good person and loyal friend.
- ☑ I am capable of achieving my goals.
- ☑ I believe in myself.
- ☑ I am motivated to make a positive impact.
- ☑ I am proud of myself.
- ☑ I am destined for success and happiness.

6

Honor Your Limits

No one functions well when they're exhausted or discontent, yet American culture has normalized and even glorified the notion of being 'crazy busy.'

My daughter Jamie discovered this early in life. In her YouTube video, "My Advice as a Colorado State Graduate," Jamie speaks vulnerably about her rollercoaster ride through college—from eager and naive to savvy and sustainable.[8] With full-time classes, part-time jobs, and an executive sorority position, Jamie flung herself into university living and quickly reached her limit.

Her video talks about that relatable feeling of failing at just one thing, though it feels like you're failing at everything. That place of self-defeat led Jamie to start saying no to others and yes to herself. Jamie also sensed that if she wasn't her best self, others would be impacted. Even when her tensions were not verbally expressed, they were likely felt.

One of my signature statements is "You are your own billboard." You project a message, not only at school or at work, but everywhere you go—in the parking lot and in your car, basically everywhere, online and offline. Not only are you being noticed, you are adding your vibe everywhere you go. We've all walked into a room and felt someone's stress. It can be easy to lose awareness of how we come across, and I love that Jamie was able to catch herself, consider the impact on others, and self-correct.

Do you know what your body language, virtual presence, and overall vibe is saying? While it's true, people judge each other according to their bias and moods, we do have some control over our public presentation.

> **What do you need to feel and look your best?**
> **How can you set more boundaries to achieve that?**

Perhaps the best version of you only returns emails from 9 a.m. - 5 p.m. or only has energy for one networking event per week. Maybe you like being in small groups of people, rather than large crowds. Can you give yourself permission to go to bed earlier?

Say yes to you!

See what you can limit or eliminate to strengthen your happiness and health. And be honest about who and what needs to go. Finding peace means knowing, honoring, and sometimes overreaching your boundaries. Let your limits be where they are and be thankful to be in communication with them.

7

Keep Your Eyes Up

Office culture has drastically shifted in recent years. We now have remote work, hybrid offices, and necessary technology. As a result, people are expected to be tied to their phones 24/7, or so they believe.

In a meeting with executives, one VP raised his hand when I mentioned our dependence on technology. He said it's not uncommon for his phone to blow up while he's at church. His company receives hundreds of emails on Sunday, and though it's set to auto reply, he said it is impossible not to peek when his phone is vibrating nonstop in his back pocket.

Lack of boundaries with technology is a massive issue in our culture. People want to be available. They want to communicate when it's convenient for them. They also want to share important news before and after work. When I question my clients why the urgency, it's often the same answer – so they don't forget.

Here's the problem with that. Even if the email you send is positive, it could still fire up an employee's brain before bedtime. It could take them out of a special family moment. It could even ruin someone's weekend because now, they can't stop thinking about work.

People get texts at all hours of the night regarding work. It's never ending–clients, vendors, teammates, and solicitors. My clients share stories about people sending emails on Friday night intentionally, as a form of power and control. This dysfunctional form of communication has to stop.

It happens on social media too. I've received direct messages on LinkedIn during major holidays and weekends. Not only am I "not interested" in buying from them, I also wonder if they're being unkind to themselves. In their attempt to build up their business, are they putting people off and not honoring their own time?

This topic is somewhat controversial. Some think it's each person's right to work when they want. They'll argue that it's each person's responsibility not to look at their phone or laptop. That's fair and it's valid, however, let's get real about the numbers.

Gallup says 70% of their responders want to receive fewer emails, which isn't a surprise, but Gallup also says that only 50% of employees reported reading notes from their leaders.[9] This means less is more, and we need to be strategic with emails. We'll talk more about that in upcoming chapters, but for now, the point is:

People are burnt out from technology.

You can choose to turn off your phone or silence notifications to minimize distraction, although we need our phones for legitimate reasons too. That's why I suggest you don't contact people about work after work hours. Simply put, it's an intrusion on their free time to recharge, something everyone seems to be lacking and aching for.

This challenge might cause some resistance.

One of my clients, a company owner, was unwilling at first. He said he didn't expect his team to respond after hours. He, like the others, was only sending them so he wouldn't forget. He said that's when some of his best ideas arrive – after work. It's also how he decompresses from the day, by writing reminders and following up on his correspondence.

I coached him to keep doing his best writing on evenings and weekends, if he must, but schedule it to be sent on Monday at 8a.m. At first, he hesitated. Even this idea can be challenging for some because we're used to getting instant feedback and answers. I had to remind him of his impact, "When the owner of the company sends an email off-hours, it's going to be read, and people will feel like they need to respond ASAP. Be thoughtful in your timing."

What's the kindest time you could send this?

That's the question each one of us needs to ask before contacting anyone.

When you know your impact and can set this boundary, you set a strong example for others. Not only that, you reinforce the message to your brain that not everything is urgent. It can relax without the need to scroll and add to the online noise.

You know what else this means? Don't respond to work emails during vacation! Trust the autoreply to be enough and plan for emergencies. It takes discipline and courage to set communication boundaries.

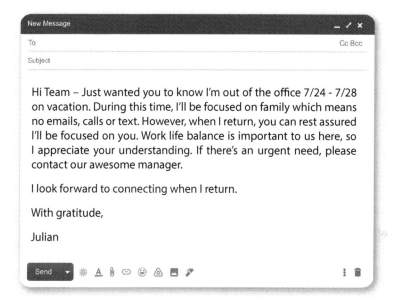

Hi Team – Just wanted you to know I'm out of the office 7/24 - 7/28 on vacation. During this time, I'll be focused on family which means no emails, calls or text. However, when I return, you can rest assured I'll be focused on you. Work life balance is important to us here, so I appreciate your understanding. If there's an urgent need, please contact our awesome manager.

I look forward to connecting when I return.

With gratitude,

Julian

One of my favorite auto-replies from Julian

Here are a few questions to get your team communication plan started:

- What is your preferred form of communication?
- Do you like face to face, email, text, instant message, phone?
- What are your preferred communication hours?
- If it's urgent, how can I get a hold of you?

With burnout and anxiety as the accepted norm, you can choose a healthier path. I've heard it said the best productivity app is to simply turn off your phone and leave it out of sight.

How can we help people do this on vacation, weekends, evenings, and even during the workday, when focus or peace are needed?

Technology addiction has become a soapbox topic for me. Because I travel for work, my time is often spent in airports. I used to love people-watching and chatting with strangers, but today, the scene has shifted.

At the Denver airport recently, a bird landed in front of a group of us waiting at the terminal. It was startling to see a bird indoors, but even more shocking that no one seemed to notice it. I looked around hoping to chuckle with someone over the bird's arrival, but all eyes were buried in screens. My phone was in hand too, so I wound up taking a picture of my new bird friend.

Bird show at the Denver airport

Do you ever worry what these tiny machines are doing to us? I sure do! Consider the current state of affairs:

- Americans check their phones 144 times per day.
- 89% say they check their phones within the first ten minutes of waking up.
- 27% use or look at their phone while driving.
- 75% use their phone on the toilet. (Ha ha!)
- 69% have texted someone in the same room as them before.
- 57% consider themselves "addicted" to their phones.[10]

These stats aren't meant to conjure shame. They're to help us stop being enablers and active participants in our own (and others') phone addiction. Think of it like this, if you had a loved one struggling with alcohol addiction, would you contribute to their struggle by offering them a drink? Of course not. Same can be said for phone addiction. Let's set some healthy boundaries and remind each other how nice it is to talk face-to-face.

That's another issue with technology – it can drive a wedge in our relationships. An innocent beep can send a signal that your technology matters more than the person in front of you. One of my clients said his Apple Watch made an unexpected ding during an important business meeting. "I could see the shock and disappointment on the other person's face. The conversation was over before I could even apologize," he said with regret. Research has shown the mere presence of a phone can be problematic. People report significantly lower connection to their conversation partners, as well as less trust and empathy, when technology is on the table or in view.

> It's rare to be with others who aren't holding their phones. That's why it's easy to stand out by putting yours away.

Let's get honest about cell phone addiction, if even for children's sake. Common Sense Media finds about half of 11 to 17-year-olds get at least 237 notifications a day. Some get nearly 5,000 in 24 hours.[11] I can't help but wonder what technology is doing to their growing brains. It's common to see kids and teens looking at their phones instead of each other, and it's concerning because they aren't learning the value of eye contact and presence.

Presence is one of the kindest gifts you can give.

"Be where your feet are," is one of my favorite sayings. That means: Put down the phone, take a deep breath, and take in your surroundings.

- If you're on a hike, be on the trail.
- If you're in a meeting, be fully engaged.
- If you're eating a meal, be with the food.
- If you're driving, be on the road.
- If you're with someone, be with just them.

Being present is about opening your senses and letting them inform you. Like the legendary spiritual teacher, Ram Dass, said, "The quieter you become, the more you can hear." Smell the soap in the shower. Feel the warmth on your skin. Watch the steam rise. Hear the water falling.

Mindfull Awareness Expedition

- ♥ Find something that reduces your stress.
- ♥ Find something you love to eat.
- ♥ Find something outside that makes you smile.
- ♥ Find something with three colors on it.
- ♥ Find something you love to listen to.
- ♥ Find something you love to feel.
- ♥ Find something that makes you feel happy.

Do you have scenery, plants, or special objects that make you happy? Take notice of your surroundings, as well as the people around you, and remember that science has proven how everything we think, as well as who and what's around us, dictates how we feel.

Do your closest people drain or energize you?
Can you find solace in your home space?
Have you shown appreciation for your plants and animals?
Can you put away your phone and tune in with yourself?

Have you given gratitude to yourself and others?

When transformation starts with you, it spills over into other areas. That's why we spent this time personalizing your lifestyle. It's not pampering, nor is it indulgent. It's the foundation needed to soar in every other area of your life, namely your relationships, impact, and leadership.

Make It Personal . . .

Your Personalized Wellness Checklist:

With the distractions of daily life, it's easy to get caught up in the demands and expectations of others. We often forget to prioritize our own well-being. Slow down, take a step back, and invest time and effort in yourself before giving to others.

☑ Witness yourself honestly

☑ Imagine the finish line

☑ Feel the ideal feeling

☑ Speak your gratitude

☑ Find your life path

☑ Honor your limits

☑ Keep your eyes up

Align your team where they want to go next.

Chapter 2

Personalize Your Leadership

"A boss has the title, a leader has the people."

— *Simon Sinek*

One of the perks of my job is going behind the scenes in various industries. I've been shown the inner workings of manufacturing plants, funeral homes, tech companies, advertising agencies, car dealerships, food processing plants, and medical clinics. I've stocked shelves for my clients and have ridden on their private jets, and while their products and services vary, they all have one thing in common: They need people to succeed, and from within that culture, leaders can arise from anywhere.

Being a leader doesn't always mean you're in the highest paid positions. Everyone from the top down can be a leader. Knowing this makes leadership accessible to everyone. It's about aligning your efforts to help others succeed.

Leadership isn't about titles. It's about your ability to inspire people and cultivate strong relationships.

Too often, we wait for someone else to be the hero of change, yet anyone can be a catalyst for transformation. That's what we'll examine together in this leadership chapter, along with a careful examination of how to better relate and communicate as an established or upcoming leader.

Before we begin, take a minute to recall the kindest thing someone's ever done for you at work. I've asked this question hundreds of times. At first, the responses surprised me. I thought I'd hear stories of exceptional kindness and generosity, like people being given vacations or huge sums of money. That wasn't the case. On the whole, the kindest deeds are when people give of their time and show interest in other people.

When something wasn't going well at work:

- Someone sat down and listened.
- Someone asked about their aspirations or opinions.
- Someone saw them as human, not just an employee or company asset.

> "Attention is the rarest and purest form of generosity."
>
> —Simone Weil

Notice, these gestures were not grand, yet their impact was huge. Also notice how when people were in distress, no answers or solutions were needed. They didn't need anyone to fix or save them. They were happy just to be seen and heard – to be sat with. They wanted to be themselves, speak their mind, and to have someone say they mattered.

That, right there, is why this chapter exists!

If you've ever believed that leadership was beyond your capabilities, know that it's easier than you might think, and no title dictates who's determined a leader – the impact does. Ready to start personalizing your leadership? Let's talk about how it's done.

1

Say Their Name

I'll never forget Ken who worked at the front desk of one of my gyms. When I'd walk through the door, his smile would beam from behind the counter, as he'd shout, "Welcome, Allison!" This is standard customer service, I know, but Ken said it with sincerity and enthusiasm. I could feel his authenticity and warmth. He made me feel visible, and his greeting also motivated me back into the gym. When I wanted to take a day off, I'd joke about the travesty of letting down Ken.

He demonstrated how leadership has nothing to do with pay grade or prestige. It's about remembering someone's name and belting it out with confidence.

My McDonald's client told me about their team member who worked the delivery window in West Linn, Oregon. When she died, customers flooded to her funeral, and what they said was all the same, "She always remembered my name and my order." I bet she would have been shocked to know how many people were profoundly touched by her remembering their names, as well as their special orders.

She created a legacy of making people feel special.

"To the world you may be one person, but to one person, you may be the world."

—Dr. Seuss

Are you cringing right now because you always seem to forget people's names? Guess what? You're far from alone. This is a common mental block, although it's not a permanent one. Forgetting names is not a lifelong sentence! With a little belief in yourself, you can change this quality and become a name-recalling superstar. Are you up for the challenge?

Name tags are always helpful.

Okay, here are some tricks:

While speaking at a retreat with HDR Engineering, I challenged Ron, Senior Vice President, to name all 35 people in the room. He claimed there was no way, so I doubled down and bet that he could. An hour later, Ron amazed the crowd and himself, when he correctly stated 35 first and last names.

What led to this incredible feat? Ron's belief in his own abilities, and the power of the mind to achieve the impossible.

Remember, your brain is programmed to believe what you tell it, so I first had to convince Ron that he could do it. He then read through my five-step process for remembering names, which helped his mind begin to shift. I'll never forget the shock on his face when he pulled it off. It has been over a decade, and we still laugh about it today.

Here's the cheat sheet I gave to him:

5 Steps to Remembering People's Names

1. Stop thinking about yourself and focus on the other person.
2. Really listen to their name. Be Fully present.
3. Ask them to repeat it if you didn't hear or understand what they said.
4. Repeat it to yourself and back to them.
5. Create a picture in your mind that links to their name.

Step five takes some explaining. Allow me to elaborate:

To help us remember his name, my client, John Colby, told us to envision him coming out of a port-a-potty (John) carrying a cheese platter (Colby). We all laughed, but it was effective. You could imagine someone named Carol to be singing holiday tunes, or Mike could be holding a large microphone. Ken could be remembered by conjuring up the memory of a Ken doll.

When people have challenging names, it's not uncommon for them to be passed over or ignored, both online and in person. Do your best to make sure everyone's included with their name spoken clearly. And it's okay to ask for help with pronunciation, even if you have to ask more than once.

For unfamiliar sounding names, try the "sounds like" game. A client once explained that his name was Updesh, but that he liked to be called Uhoop. To easily remember, he said to think of the famous song from the nineties, "Whoomp! (There it is!)" This made his name both unforgettable and fun to say.

Another way to remember names is to link them to someone you know. One of my former neighbors had the same name as my daughter. Each time I saw her, Jamie popped into mind too. Then, there's Steve, who I met at the gym. To remember his name, I envisioned Stevie Wonder working out next to him on the elliptical. That visual worked for me every time and also kickstarts a "very superstitious" playlist in my head.

By taking the time to remember names, you show people they have value. You show them you care. It's a small, but effective way to personalize your interactions and strengthen your leadership.

2

Learn to Make Small Talk

Now that you're practicing the art of presence, listening, and believing, let's examine how you're stepping into conversations with different people.

I've always been the kind of person who is friends with everyone. Even in high school, I didn't join cliques or fit in with just one group. I'd roam between the jocks, brainiacs, cheerleaders, and drama kids—and it's still the same today. Strangers often become instant friends. These connections quickly progress because I place the focus on them, rather than talking about myself.

> "There are no strangers here, only friends you haven't yet met."
> — W.B. Yeats

"Be more interested than interesting" is an evergreen principle of Dale Carnegie. In essence, he's asking, how much can you get to know people without needing reciprocation? Can you give them your full attention? Can you leave without saying a word about yourself?

This is one of my favorite social challenges – to say very little and get people talking about themselves.

Now, here's the thing, we all need to be heard and validated at times. That includes the one who's listening, although it's often a relief for me to turn my focus outward and learn what's interesting about others. It only takes a few minutes to ask a few relationship-enhancing questions before people will be off and running with their stories, thoughts, and opinions.

Where did you grow up?

What song gets you fired up?

What do you like to do outside of work?

What's your favorite movie?

What kind of foods do you love?

According to experts, curiosity is emerging as a critical skill for success; however, a study by Harvard Business School uncovered that only 24% of employees report feeling curious at work. That means that the vast majority of workers are missing out on the benefits of asking questions and probing deeper. Plus, they're likely seen by others as followers, not leaders.

What's more, the article continues, 70% said there are barriers that prevent them from asking more questions.[1] Pressure to perform, fear of judgment, or threat of punishment can quickly shut down a curious mind and stifle communication.

Thankfully, we have new role models for leadership!

Take the character Ted Lasso, for example. In the hit TV series, this U.S. football coach becomes a U.K. football coach with no previous experience. To get trust with his players, he had to make small talk. He joked, laughed, cried, listened, and eventually, they won games together.

If you're a fan of the show, you might remember the dart episode where Rupert challenges Ted to a high stakes game at the bar. As he threw the final, victorious dart, Ted repeated his motto, "Be curious, not judgmental." It was the pinnacle moment of the episode and a keen reminder to ask thoughtful questions, and let yourself be surprised who you discover.

Now Listen, Really Listen

When I recently googled the word "listening," I found images of people wearing headphones and earbuds. This struck me as a troubling sign of the times. Listening, in its purest sense, isn't about shutting off the world and disconnecting. It's about connecting more fully!

Have you noticed how no one actually teaches us how to listen? In childhood, being a good listener is usually about compliance, but in adulthood, listening is more about setting your own needs aside. To do it well, you have to be present, hear what the person is saying, and then try to understand their perspective.

Listening well and getting curious is essential to every leader's toolbox. It's also a crucial soft skill to have. More than anything, listening is an easy way to stand out and make others feel like they matter. Remember, it's uncommon to find people who actively listen well.

Listening well takes awareness and belief in yourself. Those who listen well set the bar with their ability to make people feel cherished. Listening well also takes reminders. That's why I always offer these tips for people and challenge them to put it somewhere as a visual reminder.

Use these to prepare for your daily interactions.

10 Ways to Sharpen Your Listening Skills

1. Stop. Drop. Goal – Stop what you're doing, drop what's distracting, and become an attentive listener.

2. Choose your environment – Find the best place to have a conversation. Consider privacy and sound levels.

3. Look at the speaker – Your eye contact will indicate that you're with them 100%. Eye contact also builds trust.

4. Turn off your thoughts (and your phone) – Put your worries aside and practice being present. Concentrate on the speaker's words. Be where your feet are.

5. Use open body language – Uncross your arms and legs. This will put the speaker at ease and keep them talking.

6. Restate words and messages when appropriate – "What I heard you say was that we're moving forward with the project on Monday."

7. Ask open-ended questions – "Tell me more about that." "What was the highlight of your weekend?" These inquiries will elicit more than a yes-no response.

8. Train your eyes to see nonverbal signs – Look for signs of discomfort, like fidgeting, looking at their phone, or turning away with their feet.

9. Be patient – Let the other person finish their comment before you formulate your response and speak.

10. Remember your impact – Your time and attention are what people will remember after you're gone.

Spend a few minutes reviewing these steps each morning. Visualize yourself being present, aware, curious, and receptive. The next step is to fully take notice of the unique person in front of you.

4

Ask Questions for Connection

When we meet new people, we tend to go on autopilot and ask the same standard questions:

- "How's the weather?"
- "Are you married?"
- "Do you have children?"
- "What do you do for a living?"
- "Where do you live?"

Asking cookie-cutter questions is a missed opportunity to get to know someone. Standard questions give standard responses. Be honest, who answers honestly when asked, "How ya doing?" And who truly listens after they ask the question? Leaders don't settle for superficiality. They consciously activate their curiosity and take time to ask thoughtful questions.

We can also unintentionally offend people with these questions. Not everyone is married with children, nor do they aspire to be. That's why it helps, when stepping into conversations, to have a few high-quality questions in mind.

- What are you excited about these days?
- What's good in your life right now?
- What did you do for fun this week?
- What shows are you into?
- What books or podcasts do you like?
- What are your hobbies?
- What kind of music do you enjoy?
- What are your favorite foods?
- What's your favorite concert or sporting event?

- Tell me about your pets.
- Take any cool trips lately?

These questions aren't just for rapport building, they also build trust. When people realize they like the same things, their defenses drop and their judgments will often quiet down. People see each other as more similar than different.

Here's a perfect example of the impact commonality can have:

There was an attendee in my training who was nearing retirement and disinterested in participating, although the company required it. After multiple sessions, I casually mentioned my Colorado roots and love for the Denver Broncos. Right then, everything changed for this guy. He darted to the front of the room when we finished, proudly showing me the Broncos logo tattooed on his right ankle. His perception of me changed quickly, and he became more engaged in our sessions after our football connection.

Even a small, shared interest can make a difference. It creates a positive vibe that puts people at ease. Psychologist Shawn Achor says we're 31% more productive and 37% better at sales when our brain is in a positive state.[2]

Better answers can also be found by asking unconventional or even just direct questions. Have you asked employees what they need to do their jobs better? Have you asked customers how to improve their experience? These don't have to be formal conversations. When it's casual and impromptu, people will be more likely to speak freely.

> Ask what people are thinking, feeling, and wanting. They might have a solution no one else has been able to pinpoint.

5

Find What Makes Them Special

Now that you have skills for remembering names, listening well, and asking great questions, let's discuss how to see people's true nature. After all, leadership requires you not to see people as stereotypes, but rather as unique beings with their own set of skills, desires, and needs.

Have you ever taken standardized assessments like DISC, CliftonStrengths, Myers-Briggs, or the Enneagram? These tests can feel like you've been given a map of your brain, and they're helpful in getting to know others too. I took my first assessment in my 20s and was hooked. Discovering the personalities, motivations, and communication styles of those around you, as well as your own, can be a game-changer for your leadership.

For instance, some people are brilliant big picture thinkers, but struggle with fine details—and the opposite is true as well. These tests allow you to identify and work with your strengths and opportunities for improvement, instead of feeling ashamed or frustrated. They also give us more patience and understanding of others, which once again, is a key characteristic of leadership. Suddenly, you realize those quirks and tendencies you thought were flaws are just aspects of a person's personality.

For decades, I've been using personality assessments as a coaching tool for clients, and so far, only a few have said their results seemed off. They felt more appreciated for their strengths, accepted for their shortcomings, and propelled to make change.

Granted, personality tests don't take race, gender, and other power dynamics into consideration, yet they can help bridge communication and help people better reach their goals. In some cases, these test results will reveal the potential for a different career path. A good leader can help people make those transitions.

If you or your team has never taken one of these assessments, ask for it. The more self-aware you are as a leader, the more effective you'll be. You'll also gain valuable wisdom about each person's uniqueness.

Another way to reveal something unique is through the question: What's something you've done outside your comfort zone? (One that's appropriate to tell, of course!) I like to ask this question at leadership retreats and have everyone break into groups. After stories are swapped, the top vote getter is chosen to talk about their experience with the group.

At one retreat, a woman named Elaine had the best story. As she described an 800-mile road trip with her partner on their motorcycles, we all sat there floored by this quiet, petite, conservatively dressed woman, who had cruised the open roads on a motorbike.

That wasn't even the best part:

She said they visited a place called the Sourdough Saloon in Northwestern Canada, where the Sourtoe Cocktail is a long-standing tradition. To participate, you have to buy a shot that includes a dehydrated, human toe at the bottom of the glass. Elaine and her partner willingly obliged. They ordered Yukon Jack and slammed their shots as the toe hit their lips.

The Sourtoe Cocktail, Richard Galloway

The Sourtoe Cocktail Club dates back to the 1920s, when a rum-runner named Louie Linken and his brother Otto had to take an ax to Louie's frozen big toe. To keep it preserved, they stored it in a liquor jar. After Louie's toe was discovered by Captain Dick Stevenson, this club and unconventional tradition was created. Since then, over 25 toes have been acquired by donation.[3]

When Elaine finished her story, the whole room was in shock, then we erupted with laughter. She paved the way for others to show their humanity, quirkiness, bravery, and sense of humor.

Above all, her story built trust with her teammates. Every whiskey lover, Canadian traveler, and motorcycle enthusiast in the room was fist-bumping and chatting with Elaine afterwards. She actually made herself a legend that day!

6

Discover Their Unique Needs

As a leader, you must familiarize yourself with the people you're leading, so you don't risk alienating those who may be different from you. Yes, that means discovering their areas of opportunity and strengths, but also knowing how to personalize their needs.

Here are some tips to be more inclusive in your leadership.

a. **Account for different motivations** – Leaders often forget that not everyone is motivated the same. Everyone has different motivation styles that can change from hour-to-hour and day-to-day.

I recently heard a Huberman Lab podcast that said, if you're struggling with motivation and procrastination, you should consider the potential negative consequences of not reaching that goal, or what might go wrong if you don't take action. This approach can stimulate bodily responses, such as the release of hormones, which can help kick-start motivation.[4] I like this distinction because it gives people a chance to feel what they feel, so they can shift into action appropriately.

b. **Account for neurodivergence** – Each of us is unique in the way we perceive the world and process information. Being neurodivergent means having a brain that works differently from the average or "neurotypical" person. Some examples include people with ADHD, autism, or dyslexia. These diagnostic labels explain diverse ways of thinking, learning, processing, and behaving. In short, there's no right way to process information; differences are not deficits. On the contrary, they are what make individuals unique.

c. **Personalize environments for disabilities** – One of the worst assumptions you can make is that everyone is able-bodied. Make sure to customize your environment for people with disabilities. Questions to ask: Is this space set up for wheelchair accessibility? What about people who are blind, deaf, or hard of hearing? Does anyone in your audience need braille or sign language?

"Disability only becomes a tragedy when society fails to provide the things we need to lead our lives - job opportunities or barrier-free buildings, for example. It is not a tragedy to me that I'm living in a wheelchair."

— Judy Heumann

d. **Be relatable to everyone** – While giving a presentation, I once talked about flying on an airplane and asked, "Hey, who has a great plane story?" I quickly realized 60-70% of my audience had never been on an airplane. It was a reminder that not everyone has had the opportunity to fly. Once again, get to know your audience before saying things that might alienate people.

e. **Don't assume everyone drinks alcohol** – In the workplace, alcohol mustn't be the basis of fun and inclusion. One of my coaching clients worked for a company that had free flowing cocktails and regular happy hours. As a nondrinker, it was uncomfortable because she didn't drink, and she also feared it held her back from opportunities to advance. Her instincts were spot on. Off-site team building events can build camaraderie; however, they should never exclude anyone.

When I lived in Reno years ago, I brought a treat and bottle of wine to welcome new neighbors. I was embarrassed to discover they were members of the Church of Jesus Christ of Latter Day Saints, a religion that urges members not to drink. Lesson is: Alcohol is not a universal gift.

7

Evoke Their Happy Place

To build trust and commonality, I'll ask training participants to partner up, grab their phones, and find three pictures that make them happy. It can work virtually too. Just choose an image to hold up to the screen. It's really fun to see the variety. People are proud of their cars, families, pets, and their plates of food. They show pictures from vacation, home projects, and cool adventures that they've had.

When we're done, I always ask, "Did you learn anything new about the people you work with every day?" The answer is always yes.

This exercise prompts us to change the story we've created in our brain about who someone is, or what they're all about. We're all judgmental, we all have unconscious biases, yet these exercises provide context for connecting and relating both inside and outside of work. It allows us to see the good in each other and the humanness of one and all.

> Happiness grows when we can see the good in each other.

Remember, a title or salary doesn't make a leader. It's a person's ability to connect with people and to inspire them, or at least to make them feel heard and seen. All of this is done without sacrificing your own needs!

Make It Personal . . .

Your Personalized Leadership Checklist:

Be the one to seek what's unique and interesting about others. Listen to them as though they're the only person in the room, and gather people together to find joy, commonality, and community. Leaders can set this tone, and it can happen at work, home, and everywhere. This is how legacies of leadership are built.

☑ Say their name

☑ Learn to make small talk

☑ Now listen, really listen

☑ Ask questions for connection

☑ Find what makes them special

☑ Discover their unique needs

☑ Evoke their happy place

Plant seeds that help you grow.

Chapter 3

Personalize Your Business Impact

"Great communicators don't start with what they know; they start with what the audience knows."

— *Jeff Bezos*

In a time where our attention is pulled in a million directions, consider these jarring statistics. At any given minute:

- 500 hours of video are uploaded to YouTube.
- WhatsApp users send 42 million messages.
- Zoom hosts 208,000 meetings.
- Twitter users send 350,000 tweets.
- People send 188 million emails.
- Speakers give 25,000 PowerPoint presentations.[1]

Ever wonder how our brains are able to withstand all the digital noise? Actually, the brain doesn't mind. It gets bored easily and is constantly seeking options. This psychological fact is what social media companies use to keep us hooked on their platforms. The bombardment of digital noise isn't likely to go away, which makes it tough to have impact with your message.

You might be thinking, *Why even bother trying to stand out?*

It's easier than you might think. Personalizing your business impact takes a mindset reset and a roadmap for change, which you're about to receive. And the results you'll encounter with just a few simple switches will be undeniable – career growth, leadership opportunities, salary increases, credibility boosts, and the forging of new relationships at work.

First, let's quickly review:

You have the skills from Chapter 1 to take better care of yourself, and from Chapter 2, you now understand how to step into your leadership and honor each human. This next step invites you to personalize every one of your business interactions, which might sound time consuming or calculating, but it's how you gain impact.

Being able to motivate, convince, or get people's attention is a must in business. You might think it'll slow you down to personalize every touchpoint in business, or that the marketplace is already flooded. This chapter demonstrates why changing your mindset and habits are worth the strategic effort.

1

Always Be
Presenting

At a leadership retreat, I asked participants to name all the places they leave their imprint throughout the day. The list grew quickly and didn't seem to stop. We'd have a two-second pause, then someone would think of yet *another* source of communication or random place, where business impact takes place.

Here's a list of places in business where we leave our impression:

Voicemails	Fundraising
Emails	Describing services
Instant messaging	Client reviews
LinkedIn messages	Banquets and luncheons
Presentations	Recruiting
Elevator speeches	Board meetings
Sales approaches	Making introductions
Meetings and agendas	Training and instructing others
Operating machines	Coaching and mentoring
Bathrooms	Staff meetings
Elevators	Giving feedback
Brainstorming sessions	Phone calls
Proposals	Product launches
Customer service	Keynote speeches
Break room conversations	Account meetings
Teleconferences	Q & A sessions
Sales meetings	Questioning clients
Networking	Selling products
Prospecting calls	Updating superiors
Job interviews	Talking with peers
Negotiating	Convention booths
TV appearances	Hosting events

Which one of these on the list didn't you consider? Did you forget there's always someone watching you? This is a stark reminder of how important our actions (online and offline) have become. They reflect who we are and the value we bring. Every time we open our mouths, leave the house, or show up online, we are presenting. Just as every business interaction is an opportunity to personalize.

Everywhere you go and everything you say can be recorded, shared, and scrutinized. Pause and remember your impact!

There's never been a better time to get intentional about each one of your interactions. Whether sending an email, giving a presentation, running a virtual meeting, or walking down a hallway, realize how much your words matter. Even when you think no one's paying attention, your behavior sends a signal. You are the brand of your company. You represent thousands of people with your actions in public.

Once, I was hired to coach employees about the importance of aligning actions with their company brand. They brought me in after a group of employees got drunk on an airplane wearing company logos on their shirts, hats, and luggage. Behind them was a police officer, who called headquarters and reported them. It goes to show, you never know who's watching you.

Even my McDonalds client talked about customers being rude in the drive through, while driving their logoed vehicles, or belligerent people in line wearing logoed shirts. Be conscious of the energy you project and whose brand you represent!

2

Consider Your Audience

The very nature of business is to get to know your audience/customer/client/patient and learn how to serve them well. Companies can't afford to make assumptions either. They must constantly discover what is needed from everyone who interacts with the business. Dollars and cents can become top priority, although you have to stay curious about what people are thinking.

- What would customers change, if they were in charge of the place?
- What are they holding back from saying, but would appreciate you to know?
- What would make things easier or better for them?

To launch and sustain a business, everyone must do market research, and it doesn't stop there, you have to keep including the audience in every decision.

This is the primary reason Amazon has done so well.

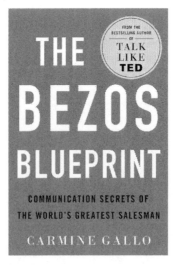

In *The Bezos Blueprint*, author Carmine Gallo says at every Amazon meeting, they designate an empty chair to represent the customer.[2] It's a reminder that the customer is always with them, influencing every refinement, consideration, and decision.

It seems like a no-brainer to get to know your customers, but you'd be surprised how resistant people can be to hearing their true thoughts. It's easier to assume we know who they are and what they want, yet there's a price to pay if we don't ask those who matter. Also, there are profits to be made by listening and adapting.

It's easy to assume you know your customers, but true success comes from listening to their unfiltered thoughts. It's about forming a lasting connection and evolving along with them—letting them become the compass from which you find your next direction.

Make
Engagement
Your Goal

Make Engagement Your Goal

How often are you in a meeting that starts late, seems chaotic, and doesn't accomplish much? I'm sure every one of you can relate. Even though we're adults, it can feel like being with children or like herding cats! That's not the fault of the people. It's up to the facilitator to get everyone on the same page.

When there's a goal to accomplish together, get in the habit of co-creating together. Ask for people's input before you create an agenda, so you can be specific and tailor it to meet their needs. "Okay, we have X number of minutes together, what do you want to get out of it?" Let their engagement pave the way.

Then, when the meeting starts, you can say, "Here's the purpose, and here is the proposed outcome of this meeting." That way, nothing is unclear and everyone can be engaged because they've contributed their needs and have a clear direction.

Have you ever received (or sent) an email that rambled on without the intention being clear? When it comes to getting buy-in from others, we think we need to dazzle them or tip toe into the subject at hand. In reality, we need to get people engaged immediately by parroting back what's urgent for them.

126   IT'S PERSONAL

Before the meeting begins, state the purpose
and proposed outcome you're hoping to
achieve.

4

Make a Good
First Impression

When you want to make someone feel welcomed, one of the easiest things to do is write out their name.

I've seen "Welcome Allison" signs at my chiropractor, as well as spas, exercise classes, and hotels. It makes me smile every time. Even my cat was recently greeted with a "Welcome Charlie" sign in the lobby of the vet. It didn't soothe his anxiety about being there, but you can bet I whipped out my phone to capture Charlie's VIP moment. This is a great practice to adopt at work. Welcome incoming hires, clients, vendors, and really *anyone*. It lets them know you're excited to see them.

Try this in your workplace.

This is why I'm a huge fan of having people's names visible. There's such value in being able to see and speak people's names. People want to be addressed as the unique individuals they are, and our names are a point of differentiation. Plus, it gets their attention and puts them in a positive state.

Once you have their attention, you have to keep personalizing. With so much information about people online, it's easy to do an informal "background check" before you meet or interact with any group or individual. This applies not only to business, but dating sites too. You will stand out to any potential partner when you notice something unique about them.

In business, we tend to look for business-related information about people, like certifications or degrees they might have. But I guarantee, that's not the most interesting part about that person, and it's not likely to get their attention either.

- *Jarod, I noticed we're both Rolling Stones fans!*
- *Dave, we pledged the same fraternity at Colorado University!*
- *Joanna, I love all the quotes you post from Brené Brown!*
- *Trihn, I admire your volunteer work at Children's Cancer Association.*

See how fun and specific these introductions are? Look for what's special about someone–like a guy I recently met who has worked for Pepsi for 25 years. Our conversation began with me saying, "I am blown away by your loyalty!" This personal touch goes a long way in building trust, standing out, and quickening connection.

On LinkedIn, do you personalize your connection requests to make them distinguishable? When I recommend this to clients, some say, "But I don't have time to dig for facts!" Doing research takes less than five minutes. I bet you've spent five minutes or more scrolling social media or playing games. If you can do that mindlessly, you can spend a few minutes getting to know someone online.

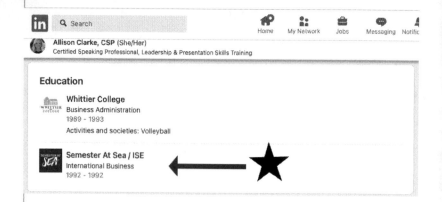

Recently, a woman on LinkedIn reviewed my profile and sent a personalized greeting. Even though her approach didn't land a sale, it was far superior to what I normally see. "Hey Allison, I saw that you did a Semester at Sea. That must have been so fun. I have an idea for your business. Could we chat?" I didn't say yes, but I did let her know that I appreciated the kind note. She made a decent first impression by pointing out something unique about my life.

Find one gem or fun fact that is intriguing and lead your greeting with that. Make people feel like you put some effort into it, and realize it actually costs you not to personalize, when a good first impression is needed. You'll easily gain rapport, productivity, credibility, and connections.

5

Give Them a Reason

Had that woman on LinkedIn given me specifics of her offer and a reason to engage, I might have taken the next step with her. But given how time-crunched we are, vague words and veiled invites won't be enough to grab people.

Listen, I'm guilty of being vague too. I'll see something cool online and quickly forward it to friends, saying, "OMG, this is great!" And while my friends might not need much convincing, it's always helpful to give people a valid reason to engage with you. Make it clear that their time won't be wasted.

Tell then WHY it's important to them!

See how these speak directly to people's interest? My point is, instead of saying, "You have to read this," you must grab people's attention. Show them why it's worth their while. What about this article, meme, podcast, webinar, or book made you think of them?

- 👌 Maria, this article had some great tips about getting nonprofit donations.

- 👌 Liam, thought you'd appreciate this guide for summer hiking.

- 👌 Ariel, I know you've been job hunting. Hope this offers some rare insights.

6

Keep it Short
and Simple

In today's complex world, people are starving for simplicity. They want to interact with brands that don't complicate the process or product.

A Harvard Business Review survey found that 63% of consumers are willing to pay more for a simpler experience, and 69% are more likely to recommend a brand because it provides simpler experiences. This explains why Google, Amazon, and even Dunkin' Donuts have continued to soar in the marketplace. They deliver hassle-free products and services that consumers want, when they want them.[3]

The need for simplicity applies to every business interaction we have.

Some of my clients, particularly compliance professionals and clinicians, often write elaborate emails that challenge people's attention span. They can't help but use technical language and big words because it's necessary in their worlds. Though when speaking to broader audiences, they forget not everyone knows their jargon, nor do they want or need all the details. I once heard about a person sending a 10-page email!

Long winded *anything* causes people to disengage and dread correspondence. You have to simplify the message in order to strengthen it. One trick is to put yourself in the shoes of someone who doesn't eat, sleep, and breathe the same information as you. Go back to the beginner's mind or wherever your target audience may be.

One way to check yourself is to use Grammarly, web based writing assistance at www.grammarly.com. It'll review your tone as well as your content to let you know how you're coming across. If you want to be friendly or direct, it'll let you know if you've achieved that. It will also check your grammar and punctuation–making your message even more readable.

Warren Buffett has a method for making his annual letter to Berkshire Hathaway shareholders both informative and digestible. He writes in an easy-to-comprehend manner, avoiding language that only industry insiders understand. But he also uses a trick to make sure he doesn't fail. He writes as though he's addressing his sisters.

"Dear Doris and Bertie," is how it begins, then he removes their names at the end. Buffet says about his sisters, "Berkshire is pretty much their whole investment." And although they're smart women, Buffett adds, his sisters are "not active in business, so they're not reading about it every day. I pretend that they've been away for a year, and I'm reporting to them on their investment."[4]

Simplicity increases what scientists call brain processing fluency. Short sentences and familiar words ensure the reader doesn't have to exert too much brain power to understand your meaning. The easier we find something to think about, the more we prefer it. It's called processing fluency, a cognitive bias in which our liking of something is directly linked to how easily our brains find it to think about, mentally process, and understand it.[5]

This makes sense, as our brain's most important job is to monitor and control our body's energy. So if you can simplify your messages and use fewer words, then you minimize cognitive strain on the reader.

People are starving for simplicity!

To learn more about shortening and strengthening your messages, check out the book *Smart Brevity: The Power of Saying More with Less* by Jim VandeHei, Mike Allen, and Roy Schwartz. It's packed with statistics and ideas that will change the way you communicate forever!

7

Sent Does not
Mean Received

At a day-long retreat for the leaders of Walsh Construction, I asked each group to read and review my listening tips, listed in chapter two. When we reached number six, "Reinforce words and messages when appropriate," I asked, "Why would it be important to restate what we heard?" Just then, a guy stood up and said emphatically, "Sent does not mean received!"

It was a mic drop moment. The room fell silent, then an outburst followed. That statement, "Sent does not mean received," meant something different to everyone. Not only does communication get easily dropped, but often, we assume it was received. But do we know for sure?

The group offered examples of emails and texts that were taken the wrong way, sent to the wrong person, and sent without deeper consideration. There's a chain of command in every industry, which means communication can be dropped at any point in the chain. Sent does not mean received, and you know what else?

Read does not mean understood!

Sent does not mean received.
Read does not mean understood.

A participant in one of my classes added this gem, and how true! Even if an email or text has been read, that doesn't mean it was taken as intended. With no body language or tone of voice, communication is largely dependent on the receiver's understanding, as well as the sender's choice in words.

I've had my own mishaps with digital communication. While reviewing outstanding invoices, I recently noticed a client still needed to pay me after 60 days. I thought, It's weird. It's not like them to be late. Well, guess what? The email that included their invoice was sitting in my drafts folder. It never went out, and it's now two months late. I couldn't figure out why the client wasn't responding, when it was 100% my fault. Has that ever happened to you before?

Did you use an incorrect email?

Did it bounce back?

Did it go to the wrong mailing address?

Is it in your drafts folder?

Did the receiver accidentally delete it?

Did your writing connect with them?

Was your email too long?

Was your subject line catchy?

Were your expectations clear?

Was accountability established?

It's a natural tendency to want to blame other people. But if they don't understand what was communicated, or they didn't receive your message, the ball's in your court to correct that. Be the one who's humble, curious, and kind, and do your best to ensure your communication comes across as intended.

Make It Personal . . .

Your Personalized Business Impact Checklist:

Given today's business climate, information overload, digital noise, and marketing mania, standing out can appear to be a daunting task. But, in truth, there's never been a better time to shine by personalizing your outreach. Take good care of yourself, get to know the people in front of you, and let personalizing be your competitive edge.

- ☑ Always be Presenting
- ☑ Consider Your Audience
- ☑ Make Engagement Your Goal
- ☑ Make a Good First Impression
- ☑ Give Them a Reason
- ☑ Keep it Short and Simple
- ☑ Sent does Not Mean Received

Fill their mailboxes, not their inboxes.

Chapter 4

Personalize Your Appreciation

"The deepest principle in human nature is the craving to be appreciated."

— *William James*

At the end of a long day of training, I will often bring people together for one final exercise. Breaking into groups, I ask them to take turns giving each other heartfelt and sincere compliments, along with a few words about why their attributes make a difference.

It's really quite a touching scene. Humble smiles, hands over hearts, and sometimes, people will break into tears. It reminds me how much we need to hear what's good about ourselves. To discover someone thinks we're funny, helpful, smart, or brave can be life changing. It can instantly and positively alter our view of ourselves.

Before they walk away, I ask who has more energy. Nearly every hand will shoot up. This training exercise is strategically placed at the end, so participants can leave on a high note. This shows everyone, particularly the leaders, how appreciation can be a cost-free and reliable source of vitality, validation, and connection. That's what people need, now more than ever, and it's what this chapter is designed to convey.

Have you ever felt undervalued and overlooked at your job?

If so, you're not alone. You'd be hard-pressed to find someone who hasn't. It's no secret that companies have historically valued profits over people and struggled to create healthy work cultures. Thankfully, times are changing.

In this new era, the question isn't whether to prioritize employees, but how. A recent survey stressed the urgency:

> **80% of employees feel like their supervisors don't recognize their efforts.**
>
> **60% of respondents said they value recognition as much as money.**[1]

These stats demonstrate why keeping talent requires more than just a competitive salary and benefits package. It's not enough to tell people they matter when they've done something well. Leaders must see the whole person in front of them and learn how to repeatedly reflect their value.

Acknowledgement is one of life's most profound acts, and when you personalize your appreciation, your relationships and reputation will improve, as will your personal and professional satisfaction.

The key, however, is to leave no one behind. Find what's extraordinary about everyone and everything. It's a skill to develop for your fellow humans, and it's a powerful habit that can transform your business and relationships.

Would you like to become a champion appreciator, but you're not sure how?

Once again, it's much easier than you might imagine. You don't have to be a prolific poet. You just have to see people. Start changing your brain to focus on what you really like about them. There's always something a person does well. Give that your attention. Let's get specific about how you express thanks, respect, and praise.

1

Use the Platinum Rule

Use the Platinum Rule

The Golden Rule stands as a timeless guide for how we should behave–treat others the way we would like to be treated. This notion is grounded in the belief that most people share a common desire for considerate treatment.

While the intention is pure, the Golden Rule can sometimes cause us to project our preferences *onto* others, instead of getting curious *about* others.

That's where the Platinum Rule comes in, coined by Dr. Tony Alessandra and Dr. Michael O'Connor, in their book by the same title. Rather than treating others as we want to be treated, we should treat them as *they* want to be treated. This shift requires us to pause and ask who is capturing our attention.

Are you centered on yourself or others?

> Platinum Rule: Instead of treating others as you want to be treated, treat them as they want to be treated.

Appreciation is meant to revere the unique nature of a person, along with honoring their distinct needs and wants. This means, once again, that you must always know your audience.

- What do they like?
- How do they prefer to connect?
- What kind of gift or act completely wows them?

Growing up, my mom was the queen of giving. She had a knack for personalizing presents that would make people melt. From her, I learned to forego my preferences as the giver and get to know the receiver. Mom was one of my first teachers to show how to be present, listen closely, ask questions, and give well.

I'll never forget our Colorado Children's Chorale conductor, Duain Wolfe. My mom caught wind that he loved Crown Royal whiskey, and so we always gave him a bottle every year for the holidays in its signature purple bag. Another recipient was my preschool teacher, who had lost her teeth and could only eat soft foods. See's Candies was her favorite. We made sure she was given the creamiest selections, as a token of appreciation.

My mom brought the same energy into organizations. The Colorado Philharmonic Orchestra had a summer camp program, where they asked community members to 'adopt' a musician. We'd find out what our adoptee liked, then we'd decorate their room and decide which places they might like to see in Colorado. My mom had a blast making people feel like they mattered.

Another core memory is of the World Almanac my dad would receive for Christmas. Mom started this tradition when they first met, and I carry it forth to this day. My father looks forward to unwrapping his Almanac from under the tree, and I look forward to watching him flip through its pages. These are moments I wouldn't trade for anything.

My sister Kate and I enjoying our birthday cake.

Birthdays were always great too. My mom gave us birthdays that were tailored to our liking. Fondue and yellow cake with chocolate frosting were my go-to selections. I actually still have (and still use) my mom's fondue set and cake knife. It's traveled with me for the last 30 years through 17 moves. They are family relics at this point and reminders for me to honor the other person's unique taste.

Considering the Platinum Rule will make your appreciation more specific. Think of giving like a wedding or baby shower registry, where the goal is to give items that are greatly wanted and needed. Aunt Ruth might be eager to buy that flamingo-shaped water pitcher, but she's better off choosing the pink retro-style blender from the registry. Like most people, she wants her gift to be cherished.

When you ask people how they would like to be appreciated, it ensures their enjoyment. My friend who works at a window and door company said they recently shifted the referral bonuses. For years, they gave team members a $150 certificate to an upscale restaurant. But then, one of the leaders questioned if the cash equivalent might be preferred for an associate with young children at home. The money could help them stock up on groceries, hire a babysitter, or to buy whatever they want, and it's what they happily accepted.

Celebrating others requires personalization, and when it's business related, the impact can be even greater. Forego the desire to appreciate how you would prefer and turn your attention to the receiver.

2

Discover Their
Receiving Style

Too often, we believe we should take whatever attention or affection we can get. When in fact, it feels infinitely better to be appreciated in a manner that means most.

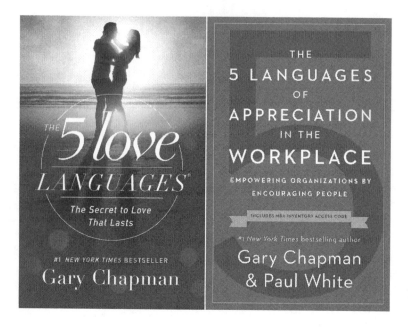

Gary Chapman is author of the bestselling relationship book, *The Five Love Languages*. This revolutionary guide swept the interest of couples across the world. Finally, people could discover what kind of love felt the best, and then request more of it.

The book *The 5 Languages of Appreciation in the Workplace* by Gary Chapman and Paul White, is another favorite of mine. It stresses the need to understand an individual's preferences for receiving recognition in a professional setting. Recognizing whether someone prefers public recognition or written compliments (Words of Affirmation), or if they value quality conversations or small group dialogues (Quality Time), or if they'd like some assistance with tasks or help at home (Acts of Service) allows for more tailored workplace appreciation.

It's fun to figure out what you prefer, but also to discover the appreciation style of those around you. Personality assessments can be helpful for this task as well. They can reveal a person's motivators and behavioral profile, but don't just guess or rely on a quiz to tell you how people like to be honored. Ask them – and let them change their minds too.

3

Appreciate All
the Time

Do you know what usually happens when a person is freshly hired? In the first 90 days, everyone's touting the company values, on their best behavior, and praising the new person. Six months later, reality sets in, and the culture reveals itself.

This commonly happens when businesses offer a special deal for new members or signing bonus. They shower you with love at first, then the accolades start to dwindle. That was my experience at a fitness class in Fort Collins, Colorado. Each time I'd visit, they'd send an email to applaud my workouts and encourage my return. They even gave me a T-shirt when my membership reached 90 days. But after that, communication from them was minimal. No more "way to go" emails or invitations to classes. No more encouragement to reach for my next goal. It's not like I was upset not to hear from them, but it was a missed opportunity to keep me involved and to say thanks for being in their community.

Praise and recognize people all the time.

I'm not suggesting you smother them, just stay consistent. That's how we know people are real and not just engaging in flattery or love bombing. Most people can sense when they're being wooed, and they can also feel when they've been forgotten. To convey your loyalty and awareness of them, stay consistent.

Acts of appreciation can be small and brief, and still be meaningful. You can reach out to a friend and say, "Thinking of you." You can put a note on your neighbor's windshield that says, "Have a great day!" As a big fan of Post-It Notes, I encourage you to jot down a brief message and go make someone's day.

- *Thanks for having my back.*
- *I couldn't have done this without you.*
- *Thank you for listening.*
- *Your humor kept us going.*
- *Thanks for being so prepared.*
- *You rocked it!*

You can try this at home too. When my daughters were in school, I'd often break out my dry erase markers and write "You got this!" on their bedroom mirrors. Now as adults, both Jenna and Jamie do this for me. They'll leave loving notes to surprise me, knowing it'll take me months to throw them away. It goes to show, if you put energy towards people, there's a chance it will come back to you.

Have you ever saved a handwritten note? I still have one from my dad from the fall of 1996 on my wedding day. Reading his words felt profound to me. The marriage didn't last, but this handwritten note is something I'll cherish forever.

To Allison   9.14.96
A gift to express my love, pride
and happiness for you. Please
know that you have made my
fatherhood experience wonderful.
Now that you go on to a next
step in life I hope you wear these
with pleasure, love Dad

Too often, we forget to show our love, until a holiday, special event, or tragedy occurs. Maybe that's why we have designated days of remembering what's good. Did you know these holidays existed?

- January 21st is Squirrel Appreciation Day

- May 14th is Dance Like a Chicken Day

- June 18th is International Picnic Day

- October 13th is International Skeptics Day

These made-up occasions are indeed real. You can google "unconventional holidays" and find nearly one for every day of the year. For me, these are stark reminders of how little we appreciate all things, all year round—so much that we need fabricated holidays and reminders of what's special in life.

- Are you grateful only on Thanksgiving?
- Are you courteous only on World Kindness day?
- Do you only love on Valentine's Day?
- Are you gentle on the planet only on Earth Day?
- Do you only give feedback at work during formal reviews?

My motto is: *If you only give your attention to people, places, and things one or two times per year, it's not enough. Giving thanks is a daily practice. If we are present and paying attention, we can appreciate all kinds of things, all the time.*

4

Say No to Automation

Right now, every social media has an automatic button, not only for generic comments and emojis, but also to say congratulations, thank you, and happy birthday. Automation may bring ease to certain tasks, but it eliminates thoughtfulness and personalization. It's simply not impactful!

Each year in mid-May, I receive at least 100 automated, direct messages on LinkedIn saying, *Happy work anniversary.* I've never met most of these people, nor do we engage or do business together. And while I appreciate the well wishes, it would have meant so much more if they had commented on my posts or personalized their message to me in some way.

It takes only seconds to name a special moment you've had together, or to appreciate someone's talents, or to share your belief in their potential. These extra words have an immense impact. Look at the person in front of you and tailor your words to them specifically.

> ★ *Happy Birthday, Hiroshi.* ★
> *Your sunrise pictures are always amazing.*
> ★ *Hey Pat, congrats on your new job.* ★
> *Your people skills are astounding!*
> ★ *Your latest promotion is well deserved, Puneet.* ★
> *Way to keep reaching for new goals!*

This goes for 'thank you's' as well. I've heard people complain about bosses who will say thanks, but never get specific. People need to hear *why* their actions matter.

- Thank you for coming in early today.
- Thank you for getting those reports done.
- Thank you for asking that question.
- Thank you for going the extra mile.
- Thank you for making things easy on me.

Adding specificity puts you in a category all alone. It's a step most people don't take. And don't forget, if you're on the receiving end of a 'thank you,' "You're welcome" is a kind and sufficient response. In that case, nothing else is needed.

When you're willing to do what others won't, you'll stand out as a leader and extend your kindness to new heights.

5

Know Their Rituals and Expectations

People spend more time at work than anywhere else, so why not have more fun in those long and sometimes tedious hours? One way is to celebrate worldwide holidays. Here's an exercise to do with your coworkers. Go through all the major holidays and describe what's important to you on that occasion. What are your expectations? Is there a food you love to make, a place you like to go, or a tradition you try to uphold?

Here are a few holidays that can be celebrated at your company or with your customers:

New Year's Day	Halloween
Chinese New Year	Thanksgiving
Valentine's Day	Ramadan
Mardi Gras	Day of the Dead
St. Patrick's Day	Diwali
Passover	Memorial Day
Hanukkah	Fourth of July
Bodhi Day	Labor Day

This exercise is helpful for planning experiences, as well as showing individualized appreciation. It's also a way to mitigate hurt feelings and disappointment. Do you know what holidays are important to others? Even if you don't share a similar passion for events as your team, colleague, or partner, it could be worth indulging them. Give them the courtesy of honoring their wishes.

Here are some fun events that companies often have:

- Potluck for the Super Bowl or March Madness
- Ugly sweater contest for the Winter holidays
- Costume contests for Halloween
- Favorite sports T-shirts on Fridays
- Team volunteering for a charity

Over decades of coaching people, I've seen these fun events grow camaraderie with teams at work, and it also helps people's marriages, friendships, and family ties. We all need people in our lives who will celebrate our traditions and passions. Be that person for others, and then let them know what your preferences are too.

Honor the Seen
and Unseen

When I trained hotel employees at the Grand Sierra in Reno, Nevada, I discovered that valets should be tipped, not only when they bring your car back, but when you hand them your keys as well. Did you know that? Housekeeping should also be tipped $3.00–$5.00 per day, however, that's not widely known either.

Tips make a big difference

I've been in plenty of unrecognized service positions over the years. That's one reason I always leave a tip and sometimes a note. People work tirelessly. Appreciating those behind the scenes should be considered a travel expense, not an option or grand gesture of kindness.

This is why I keep a treat basket on my front porch with KIND bars and bottled water for delivery drivers. When it's cold, I include hand warmers. When it's warm, I leave out cold water and

Gatorade for them. I am also vigilant about thanking cleaning crews at hotels, and really anyone who's largely unseen, but important.

Kroger, one of my long-time clients, has a stamp on every check that's sent to their associates and vendors. It says: *Highly satisfied customers made this check possible.* What a great reminder that their impact is what brought them this check. And who thinks of personalizing paychecks? Not many, yet it's a really nice tribute to each person who makes the money possible.

You can also personalize online payments. Paypal and Venmo both allow you to drop a personal note.

- *It's been an honor doing business with you.*
- *Thanks for being one of the best in the business.*
- *Your creative skills are extraordinary. Thanks for sharing them with us.*

I recently heard about a medical clinician whose PowerPoint presentation paid homage to his contributors. On each slide was an arrow naming the person responsible for the research or discovery. It's often assumed that the presenter alone has compiled their entire body of work. Yet behind every project, business, or initiative are people who deserve recognition. There's a child inside each of us who still longs to be seen and heard by someone.

Even those with multiple degrees and corner offices yearn to be appreciated. That's why it's best to name the sources that have shaped your work—the quotes and research that form the backbone of your ideas. Say the names of your mentors and influencers. It's a hat tip to them and a testament to the power of collaboration. After all, no one achieves entirely on their own.

> We are products of those around us, and our success is often the result of those relationships.

Niagara Bottling has a cool way of celebrating their collective wins. If the plant workers hit all their safety metrics for the year, their names are put into a hat for a new car giveaway. This event celebrates Niagara's employees and their dedication to safety. It's also a big investment and a big deal when the winner is announced.

Niagara's car giveaway, celebrating workplace safety

7

Always Say Thank You

Now, here's the thing—I don't ever expect people to thank me in return. That's not the motive of giving, but I'm surprised at how few people acknowledge when they've received something. Why is saying thank you difficult for some people? I'm sure it has to do with different brain styles and personalities, however, if you want to forge better relationships and adopt a personalizing lifestyle, you have to say thank you.

A text, call, or email could be enough, but in my opinion, nothing beats a handwritten note.

Snail mail is usually unwanted bills and flyers, so when you receive a card tucked in your mailbox, it's kind of a big deal. It's a nostalgic form of appreciation that doesn't get deleted or forgotten. One of my mail carriers told me that 95% of all mail gets thrown away. That's no surprise, and it shows how much a handwritten note can stand out and literally astound a person.

Be sure not to let stamps and shipping stop you from appreciating. There are other effective ways. The point is to do it. Pick up the phone, send a text, make a call, or even send an email. Just remember to personalize. Say something more than "happy birthday," "congratulations," or "way to go." Personalize your appreciation to the recipient. Give it some depth!

One of my friends does this really well. I recently sent her something from Sugarwish, a website for personalized gifting. As the giver, you select how much you want to pay and what items you want presented as options. The receiver gets notified and then gets to select from dozens of options. My friend chose from an assortment of dog treats and added a red and pink dog bowtie to the mix. When the present arrived, she promptly dressed up her dogs, snapped pictures, posted them on social media, offered her thanks, and tagged both me and Sugarwish. It felt like a win for us all, especially the dogs!

Grandiose thanks and public gratitude isn't always needed, but individual gratitude is a must. I think of it like hugging someone back or closing an open loop.

To this day, Linda takes the cake for one of the best thank you notes. After I sent her a bouquet of holiday flowers, she took a picture of them, printed a copy, added a heartfelt note, and mailed it to me. I was so blown away by her gesture, I wound up sending *her* a thank you email. That might seem unnecessary, but I just couldn't let her gesture go unnoticed. Linda made my day and created a memory neither of us will forget.

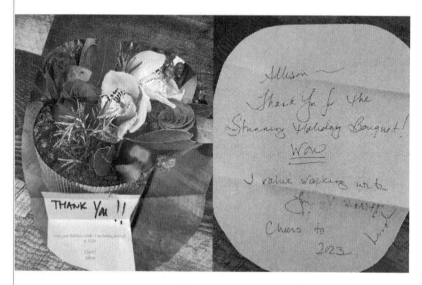

Best thank you note ever!

Another award-winning thank you was from Brian. Knowing their company mascot was a beaver and his dogs meant everything to him, I jumped at the chance to buy these hilarious squeaky beaver toys for his dogs. At the end of our coaching sessions, Brian placed a slide on the screen. It was a collage of his dogs playing with the squeaky beaver toys. It was a touching reminder of the impact of small gestures–both mine and Brian's–and the ripple effect it creates.

The power of appreciation, celebration, and respect is potent. It's astonishing to think some people have never received a heartfelt thank you card or been told what truly makes them special.

I recently met a woman who used to work at Hallmark, the greeting card company. She said birthdays at Hallmark would yield at least 50 cards from her coworkers. Now, she said, in a different industry and different time, if a coworker sends a happy birthday text, it's rare.

Another client said he'd been at the same company for 25 years, and no one ever wished him a happy birthday. At his new place of employment, they gave him a card that everyone signed and a case of the company product. It was so unexpected, this 50-something year old man broke into tears. Feeling appreciated was foreign to him in a work setting. Emotionally, it took him by surprise.

Let it be you to spread the impact of personalized appreciation. Let it be you to spark the flames of connection.

I hope these stories urge you to be the person in relationships and interactions who acknowledges others. Let it be you to spread the impact of personalized appreciation. Let it be you to spark the flames of connection.

Make It Personal . . .

Your Personalized Appreciation Checklist:

This chapter underscores the significance of consistent recognition, tailored gratitude, recognizing unseen contributions, and incorporating personal preferences in how we say thanks. This is how you cultivate the habit of personalized appreciation. Notice how it won't take long to strengthen your most important relationships and perhaps even unlock the challenging ones.

- ☑ Use the Platinum Rule
- ☑ Discover their Receiving Style
- ☑ Appreciate all the Time
- ☑ Say No to Automation
- ☑ Know Their Rituals and Expectations
- ☑ Honor the Seen and Unseen
- ☑ Always Say Thank You

Just like a highway, feedback should flow both ways.

Chapter 5

Personalize Your Feedback

"Awareness is the greatest agent for change."

— *Eckhart Tolle*

When I talk with people who have natural confidence, they seem to have one thing in common: They have people in their lives who regularly give them feedback, not only in their jobs, but with everything that's important to them–health, wealth, family, friends, and faith. This helps them reach their goals and potential, and it also has a ripple effect because this person is always evolving. People notice and are impacted.

The practice of getting feedback is common with performers and athletes, same with medical professionals and technicians. They'll spend countless hours in training and endure rigorous practice just to hit the right note, perfect their timing, or to keep someone safe and alive. Feedback helps them sense what they can't see or hear themselves. It clues them in to how they're doing and provides awareness to achieve excellence.

Daily feedback is expected in high-stakes positions, but in business, the practice of giving feedback is actually rare. It's often limited to annual or quarterly reviews, which are usually awkward for both parties. Most people have a vague idea what they've done well or need to improve, until the dreaded time arrives. This system for giving feedback needs to be updated, as people need insights about themselves all the time.

The goal of this chapter is to help you create an atmosphere where feedback is given, not as a punishment or promotion, not as a quarterly or annual review, but as a regular form of relating and team building. You'll learn how to give positive and personalized feedback the instant someone does something well. You'll also learn how to give feedback when a tough conversation is needed.

Earlier chapters focused on personalizing your lifestyle, your leadership, your business impact, and appreciation. With those lessons applied, you're now at a point where you can offer (and receive) feedback with a calm and cool presence. This chapter is your chance to step further into the role of supporting others.

Let's talk about personalizing your feedback.

1

Feedback vs. Appreciation

Feedback vs. Appreciation

The lines can be blurry between appreciation and feedback, but this distinction matters—the difference is in purpose and approach.

Appreciation involves recognizing core qualities in someone. It's an expression of gratitude. It's a response to a person's contributions and impact.

- *We couldn't have done it without you.*
- *Thank you for the time you spent on this project.*
- *It was wonderful being with you at the show.*
- *Your generosity will not be forgotten.*

Feedback is more technical. It adopts a coaching mentality, similar to what athletes receive, where it provides guidance to help individuals adjust and refine their performance.

- *Your presentation skills have really improved.*
- *Those reports are great, just add some bullet points.*
- *Cut the final paragraph and your email will be ready to send.*
- *The research you found is ideal for this project.*

Do you see the difference?

People usually find it easier to appreciate because saying 'thank you' can feel effortless, like autopilot, whereas feedback requires your presence, curiosity, and keen observations. And in many cases, feedback requires consent.

It helps to know the person already, as we discussed in previous chapters. When you know their strengths and personality, when you have established trust, you can get creative with your feedback for maximum impact.

Appreciation expresses gratitude for someone's qualities and contributions, while feedback provides specific guidance to encourage and improve performance.

Lead with Kindness

When someone says, "We have some feedback for you," what's your internal reaction? Does it conjure memories of being shamed? Do you brace yourself for criticism? Can you feel your defenses go up?

These responses are normal. People have trauma from being controlled, insulted, and demeaned by authority figures, and even by friends and family.

With that said, lots of people still want more insight and observations about how they're doing at work. Everyone can benefit from feedback, whether it's a helpful suggestion, instructional guidance, or a gentle reminder of roles and responsibilities. Despite what you might think, people don't want to be in the dark. They want to know what they do not know.

A recent Forbes article said 65% of employees want more feedback.[1] Can you guess why they aren't getting it? Meaningful feedback takes time and can be unpleasant, particularly when there's weakness in training and management. But it also goes back to human nature. Most people want to be liked, so they don't take the risk of offending someone. But in the workplace, you can't hide or pretend when a hard conversation is needed. You must put aside niceness in favor of kindness. That's another distinction you need to know:

Being nice means avoiding uncomfortable conversations, like not talking to a struggling employee about their performance issues, or ignoring bias and oppressive behaviors to maintain a "pleasant" atmosphere.

Kindness means addressing issues with the intention of helping employees reach goals, foster fairness, and gain awareness of themselves, even if it's awkward at the moment or conjures an uncomfortable response.

> Niceness leads to avoidance.
> Kindness leads to courage.

If you're doing something unintentionally, or if you're doing something incorrectly, wouldn't you want to know? If people felt upset, confused, or hurt by your words or actions, wouldn't you want to know?

If so, invite people to tell you.

Make yourself open to feedback. Change the perception of errors and mistakes to become human. We all deserve a chance to make amends and adjust our behavior. Be the one to set the bar on what "kind feedback" can look, sound, and feel like.

3

Create a Positive Environment

Christopher Voss and Tahl Raz, the authors of *Never Split the Difference: Negotiating As If Your Life Depended On It*, are respected leaders in their fields. Mr. Voss had a 24-year career at the Federal Bureau of Investigation, and he excelled as the foremost international kidnapping negotiator during his tenure. Today, he teaches businesses how to better collaborate and of course, negotiate.

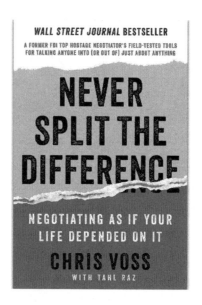

Chris always talks about building rapport with people, first and foremost. He says you must put them in a positive frame of mind to make them become more receptive, collaborative, alert, and understanding. You do this by giving them positive feedback. Tell them what they're doing well, even if they've heard it a million times.

You'd think top performers in the company would get lots of praise, but surprisingly, they don't. When a person's success is consistent, feedback given will start to decrease. You have to be sure they're commended consistently. Same is true for newbies and those who struggle. They're likely getting tons of instructional guidance, but not meaningful feedback on what's improved. As a leader, you can't let this happen.

If you've given positive feedback privately, do it publicly, in front of a bigger group, so ideas and recognition can spread.

One of my coaching clients has been making impressive strides, but felt like no one had even noticed. They were right, not one person in the company had given them positive feedback. I sent a group email, including their supervisors to highlight this person's improvements. And then privately, I coached that person's manager on how to give more positive feedback both privately and publicly.

For many, there's not much coaching needed. It's a matter of setting aside time to stop, pay attention, and find words of encouragement and support. These efforts cannot be sporadic. You need to water everyone's garden, so to speak, with specific and thoughtful feedback.

This is how solid business relationships grow, from soil that's been tended to and nourished. Giving consistent positive feedback provides a container for *any* conversation to take place, as the tough ones will inevitably follow. Welcome them, as they'll lead to more honesty, trust, and progress. Corrective coaching can turn positive when people feel safe enough to open up.

4

Name Goals
and Values

When I start coaching people, I ask them to identify what they want to focus on. In many cases, they'll give me a list of what they don't like about themselves. "Your shortcomings aren't an accurate picture of who you are," is how I typically respond. "Let's name the good, the less good, and the not so good. Or we could make a list of goals to elevate."

This wording is intentional. It's meant to help them see themselves beyond their weaknesses and remember who they are.

This conversation will inevitably lead to what actions, thoughts, and behaviors must be modified. And it's funny because most of the time, people will echo the same concerns for themselves that others have of them. I like this approach because you can avoid the risk of defensiveness. They've self-identified the things they want to correct.

At that point, your job is to lead them back to their goals and values whenever they go astray. No shame or blame necessary.

Your feedback is supporting a future vision for themselves and the company.

One of my corporate coaching clients had a situation where an employee was constantly on their phone and laptop at work summit. Their lack of attention worsened during a coveted tour of the facility. This person's disengagement sent a signal of disinterest and disrespect, and my client wanted to know if, when, and especially how they should handle this situation

The question of "if" and "when" is a no-brainer. This manager should have said something right away at the summit. It could have been no big deal. Start by not making any assumptions. Evoke your curiosity instead. Remember, we never know what people are going through.

> *Hey, I noticed you've been on your phone.*
> *Are you doing alright?*
> *Is everything okay at home?*
> *Did something happen at work?*
> *Is there anything you need help with?*

These heart-felt questions of concern are sometimes the only "feedback" people need to gain self-awareness. Depending on what's going on, they might have just needed a gentle nudge. Now if the employee said, "Nope, everything is fine," and continued to engage with their phone, then we would discuss "how" this could be (kindly) addressed.

In an ideal world, this manager would have already taken time with this employee to know their aspirations, values, and goals. "How do you want to be perceived?" is a powerful question to ask. Have each person write down their answers. Next, help them create an action plan to get those desired results. Have them put it into writing, so you can regularly review it together.

This sets up an environment where feedback is neither good nor bad, positive or negative. It's a marker to detect if a person is in line with their goals and values. You can also use this opportunity to clarify a person's expectations. "This is what you chose as an aspiration. Is that still true for you?"

Another approach to framing feedback is to use company values as a measuring stick. Let's say an employee was cutting people off in meetings. The coaching session could point to respect as one of the company's core values. From there, you can explore how the employee's actions can better align with this value. See, when you do this, feedback doesn't feel as personal or polarizing. It's simply the company code of conduct!

5

Give Specific Examples

Years ago, I was in Maine giving a kindness keynote that included pictures of the kind acts that I was doing. The reviews were positive, but one person had some critical feedback. I still remember their every word. "This presenter is in love with herself — all those photos of her and her kindness!"

Like any negative feedback, it didn't feel good, but it did cause me to contemplate. This person's feedback was not generic or broadly insulting. It didn't say, "She sucks," or "I don't like her." Their reaction was specific – when they looked at my pictures, they would have preferred to see other kind acts, not mine. Point taken!

Before my next keynote, I switched to images that would demonstrate the impact of my work. I also included examples of other people's kind acts. And you know what? It's a much better keynote now with those changes. That critical feedback was helpful because it was specific, and even though it wasn't delivered respectfully, it spurred improvement on my end.

When you're faced with the challenge of choosing your words, give the gift of kindness and specificity in your feedback.

× **Don't say "That's interesting."**
✓ **Name what's interesting about it.**

× **Don't say, "Great job."**
✓ **Find words that explain what was great.**

× **Don't say, "You're not getting it."**
✓ **Clarify what needs to be adjusted.**

People crave feedback that isn't generic, and they want it to be personalized. We all deserve to be given feedback that is tailored just for us. This goes for all employees and vendors, and even those in management and executive positions.

Everyone needs specifics on how they're actually doing. No position is exempt.

6

Feedback Goes Both Ways

In business, feedback is usually delivered from the top down, but the best leaders make sure that feedback can go both ways: from managers to employees and from employees to managers.

It only makes sense to keep these channels of communication open, although it's hard for most people to deliver difficult feedback to a boss or superior. In these instances, it's the responsibility of leaders to make it easy and safe. It's also the responsibility of the person in power to be calm, receptive, and curious. Leadership requires this kind of presence from them, as does the company's success.

Kansas City Chiefs head coach Andy Reid has a brilliant way of encouraging feedback from his players. He assigns one player from each position to collect everyone's concerns. Reid then holds what he calls "player leadership committee meetings," where each leader speaks for his group.

Former Kansas City linebacker Derrick Johnson told ESPN, "Whenever we started the meeting, the first thing Reid would say was, 'All right, what gripes do you have?'" In this open forum, anything was fair game. The players could grumble about practices, game strategy, coaching approaches, cafeteria food, or whatever else was on their minds.

Research shows that when employees feel empowered to voice concerns and share new ideas, they become up to 50% more productive.[2] Similarly, when employees feel uncomfortable voicing honest opinions and concerns, it is often a sign of dysfunction.

Reid's meetings gave players permission to vent. They also gave Reid insight into how to make improvements.

"When players said they were wearing pads too long and running too many plays at practices, Reid immediately changed his practice formats," Johnson said. "It was that quick. Most of the things we brought to him, he trusted just like that."

By swiftly addressing concerns and distractions, Reid freed up his players to focus on the essentials during practice weeks. Johnson added about Reid, "He doesn't want us to have any excuses for not getting it right on Sunday."[3]

It's the leader's role to do whatever's necessary to get people talking. Workers and football players alike are on the front lines. They have keen knowledge about what they need, what they like, and what it's going to take to succeed. That information has to find its way to management. It's often the key to greater success for one and all.

7

Be Responsive to All Feedback

Since we talked about maintaining company values, it's only natural to discuss reputation management. When you're confronted with feedback that you don't agree with or that you know you need to fix, it's okay to step back and make a plan. Take a deep breath and say, "Thank you for bringing this to my attention. May I have a moment to process this?"

Then confide in a friend, colleague, HR person, or therapist to help you gain clarity. But don't wait too long. Difficult feedback should be handled swiftly. Online, the rule of thumb is: reply to all reviews, both positive and negative, and do it quickly. If you are responsive, you can recover.

Nearly 9 in 10 respondents are more likely to overlook a past negative review, if they see the business has responded and addressed the issue. This complements a Yelp finding that customers are 33% more likely to update a critical review if a business replies with a personalized message within 24 hours.[4]

Responsiveness shows that a company is listening to their customers and employees, and is willing to admit mistakes and grow. This assures people that their feedback matters. It shows that you care enough to make it right for them. If the customer's negative experience warrants it, you can go beyond an apology and offer a refund or discount. Doing this shows people that you take negative experiences seriously and are willing to put your money where your mouth is.

I had a terrible experience recently with one of the airlines. They had us stuck on the runway in Denver for two hours, causing my next flight to be missed, due to what they said was "a communication problem with their maintenance team." I had an urgent work engagement in Florence, South Carolina, so I had to hire a driver at the airport, which was quite expensive.

When I provided feedback to the airlines, I wasn't expecting a refund, but they only offered me $25 as compensation. This was both inadequate and disrespectful considering the inconvenience faced. The airline industry is notorious for inconsideration like this. It served as a reminder for me to choose another airline moving forward.

I heard the Four Seasons hotel gives their employees a $2,500 budget for guest compensation, or they did at one time. If someone had a negative experience at the spa or in the dining room, if the pool wasn't to their liking, or the conference room was too hot or cold, the guest could be given adequate financial compensation, or at least a significant gift certificate. This empowers each worker not to fear uncomfortable feedback, but to respond appropriately without having to get permission. They just dip into their compensation budget.

This kind of resilience creates an atmosphere of positive feedback, as nothing can be deemed "bad," because accountability is sure to follow.

Make It Personal . . .

Your Personalized Feedback Checklist:

When delivered poorly, feedback can cause stress, damage self-esteem, and in some cases, ruin careers. When delivered adeptly, feedback can push people and organizations to achieve excellence. It's bonding and relationship building, and it will make you stand out in the marketplace. These seven principles can be applied to any area of your life.

- ☑ Feedback vs. Appreciation
- ☑ Lead with Kindness
- ☑ Create a Positive Environment
- ☑ Name Goals and Values
- ☑ Give Specific Examples
- ☑ Feedback Goes Both Ways
- ☑ Be Responsive to All Feedback

Conclusion

Dear Reader,

If you take away one thing from this book, let it be this: We have no idea what is happening in people's lives, and it's easy to underestimate our power to create positive change. Through personalization, you will stand out, ignite your creativity, nurture self-love, build strong connections, make groundbreaking discoveries, grow your business, and become known as a leader who elevates the quality of life. You now have tools to explore and harness your true potential.

- ★ **Personalize Your Wellness:** You delved into unconventional, yet highly effective strategies to prioritize inner peace and mental health, and to set better boundaries with technology.

- ★ **Personalize Your Leadership:** You reframed your understanding of leadership, recognizing that titles and salaries don't make leaders. True leaders connect with and inspire others, making them feel heard and seen.

- ★ **Personalize Your Business Impact:** You explored the importance of every word and action in your professional life and grasped how to stand out and make connections in a crowded digital landscape.

- ★ **Personalize Your Appreciation:** You learned how to express gratitude in meaningful ways and were reminded to acknowledge those who might be less visible, but equally deserving of recognition.

★ **Personalize Your Feedback:** You gained skills to create an environment where positive feedback is a catalyst for personal and professional growth, and a safe foundation for harder conversations

As a person dedicated to personalization, you now have the power to awaken others—not just to your brilliance, but to their own. Show them the beauty and importance within themselves, and witness how it enriches your own life as well.

Illuminate the path toward a brighter, more compassionate world. Carry forth with kindness and create your legacy, wherever you go.

It's personal, and it's all that remains.

With gratitude and respect,

Notes

Notes

INTRODUCTION

1. https://www.forbes.com/advisor/business/effective-communication-workplace
2. https://www.gallup.com/workplace/285674/improve-employee-engagement-workplace.aspx
3. Jim VandeHei, Mike Allen, and Roy Schwartz, Smart Brevity: The Power of Saying More with Less. (New York, NY: Workman Publishing Company, 2022), 2.

CHAPTER ONE

1. https://www.forbes.com/sites/christinecomaford/2012/04/04/got-inner-peace-5-ways-to-get-it-now
2. https://hbr.org/2002/06/hidden-minds
3. https://restoic.com/blogs/blog/what-is-visualization-how-successful-access-practice-this-proven-technique
4. https://www.scientificamerican.com/article/how-did-water-get-on-earth/
5. https://www.usgs.gov/special-topics/water-science-school/science/water-you-water-and-human-body
6. https://masaru-emoto.net/en/masaru/
7. https://kindlips.com
8. https://www.youtube.com/watch?v=LQEHWpc8iVw

9. Jim VandeHei, Mike Allen, and Roy Schwartz, Smart Brevity: The Power of Saying More with Less. (New York, NY: Workman Publishing Company, 2022), 138.

10. https://www.reviews.org/mobile/cell-phone-addiction/

11. https://www.nbcnews.com/health/health-news/teens-inundated-phone-prompts-day-night-research-finds-rcna108044

CHAPTER TWO

1. https://hbr.org/2018/09/the-business-case-for-curiosity

2. https://www.ted.com/talks/shawn_achor_the_happy_secret_to_better_work/

3. https://dawsoncity.ca/listing/sourtoe-cocktail-club/

4. https://www.youtube.com/watch?v=CrtR12PBKb0

CHAPTER THREE

1. Carmine Gallo, The Bezos Blueprint: Communication Secrets of the World's Greatest Salesman. (New York City: St. Martin's Press, 2022)

2. https://www.inc.com/john-koetsier/why-every-amazon-meeting-has-at-least-one-empty-chair.html

3. https://hbr.org/2015/11/why-simple-brands-win

4. Carmine Gallo, The Bezos Blueprint: Communication Secrets of the World's Greatest Salesman. (New York, NY: St. Martin's Publishing Group, 2022), 24.

5. https://sparkemotions.com/2020/05/14/processing-fluency/

CHAPTER FOUR

1. https://www.cnbc.com/2016/05/11/recognition-is-the-secret-weapon-every-leader-must-use-yum-chair.html

CHAPTER FIVE

1. https://www.forbes.com/sites/victorlipman/2016/08/08/65-of-employees-want-more-feedback-so-why-dont-they-get-it
2. https://everyonesocial.com/blog/employee-empowerment/
3. https://www.cnbc.com/2023/02/08/how-kansas-city-chiefs-coach-andy-reid-builds-trust-with-players.html
4. https://searchengineland.com/9-in-10-customers-more-likely-to-overlook-a-negative-review-if-the-business-responds-adequately-yelp-says-377004

Acknowledgments

Acknowledgments

I am grateful to everyone in my life who made me feel important by personalizing their interactions with me. This project wouldn't have happened without the partnership of Erin Donley and the challenge she presented me to keep publishing books. Thanks also to my mastermind group whose feedback and support helps me to continuously grow.

And to you, thank you for taking time to read this book and for pausing to remember your importance and impact on other people.

It's personal, and it's all that remains.

Author Bio

Since 1994, Allison Clarke, CSP, has been solving communication problems for companies and teaching the power of kindness. She's helped professionals around the globe to break through barriers and get results that improve their productivity, profitability, and personal happiness.

As a "Top 25 Master Trainer" for Dale Carnegie Corporation, Allison spent 16 years witnessing miraculous transformations. This gave her the foundation needed to launch Allison Clarke Consulting. Her client list includes Intel, Kroger, Transamerica,

Niagara Bottling, Trident Seafoods, Hanger Clinic, Reser's Fine Foods, and Dignity Memorial. These diverse companies have one thing in common–they know the success of their companies depends on their people.

Allison's first book, *What Will They Say? 30 Funerals in 60 Days*, is a study of leadership and what it means to be memorable. Her second book, "The Kindness Habit: 5-Steps to Maximize Your Happiness & Impact," offers concrete steps to leave a legacy of grace and to make a difference in people's lives.

Allison served as President of the Oregon National Speakers Association, and in 2016, she earned the CSP™ (Certified Speaking Professional), a designation that's based on criteria only 12% of speakers worldwide have been able to meet.

Allison lives in Colorado. She has two daughters and is an avid hiker, traveler, and sunrise enthusiast.

AllisonClarkeConsulting.com

Made in the USA
Middletown, DE
21 August 2024

59009439R00149